Allum's
ANTIQUES
ALMANAC
2015

Allum's ANTIQUES ALMANAC

2015

An annual compendium of stories and facts from the world of art and antiques

MARC ALLUM

ICON

Published in the UK in 2014 by
Icon Books Ltd, Omnibus Business Centre,
39–41 North Road, London N7 9DP
email: info@iconbooks.com
www.iconbooks.com

Sold in the UK, Europe and Asia
by Faber & Faber Ltd, Bloomsbury House,
74–77 Great Russell Street,
London WC1B 3DA or their agents

Distributed in the UK, Europe and Asia
by TBS Ltd, TBS Distribution Centre, Colchester Road,
Frating Green, Colchester CO7 7DW

Distributed in Australia and New Zealand
by Allen & Unwin Pty Ltd,
PO Box 8500, 83 Alexander Street,
Crows Nest, NSW 2065

Distributed in South Africa by
Jonathan Ball, Office B4, The District,
41 Sir Lowry Road, Woodstock 7925

Distributed in India by Penguin Books India,
7th Floor, Infinity Tower – C, DLF Cyber City,
Gurgaon 122002, Haryana

Distributed in Canada by Publishers Group Canada,
76 Stafford Street, Unit 300
Toronto, Ontario M6J 2S1

ISBN: 978-184831-734-5

Typeset in Van Dijck by Marie Doherty

Printed and bound in the UK
by Clays Ltd, St Ives plc

For all those who care – thank you.

Your words in my memory are like music to me.
—SNOW PATROL

ABOUT THE AUTHOR

Marc Allum is a man with serious time-management issues. Always over-employed but largely unemployable, he walks an overstretched tightrope of impossible curiosity, a perpetual chronically jammed cerebral inbox of insatiable idiosyncratic desire while desperately trying to balance this with a combination of 'real' work that pays the bills and several strangely fulfilling hobbies – actually, his main problem is the continual creation of more openings into the labyrinth of object and association: the guitar and the player, the shotgun and the shooter, the engine and the mechanic, to name just a few. Marc is on a Thesian mission to meet the past he was never able to inhabit and his life as a BBC *Antiques Roadshow* specialist, author and consultant allows him to unwind just a little bit more of that never-ending thread.

CONTENTS

Contents

Contents

Contents

Contents

Contents

INTRODUCTION

Contrary to what you might think, the obvious attraction of writing a book called *Allum's Antiques Almanac* was not a clever publishing ploy to cash in on the alliterative qualities of the three words; rather, the idea stemmed from my fervent interest in devising a format based on my interest in art and antiques and an historically appropriate vehicle for conveying a whole raft of time-sensitive facts (and some fictions). Among my varied collections are several almanacs, a type of publication originally dating back some several thousand years that came to be characterised by collections of ephemeral information such as lunar and solar predictions, horoscopes and eventually more concrete facts and figures that might aid a person in everyday life. The compilation of such material is in fact a very English phenomenon and became more popular in the late 14th century. By the 17th century such publications had become so popular that they were only outsold by that number one bestseller, The Bible. So the idea that these miniature, often beautifully embossed and tooled leather-bound publications in their similarly decorated protective leather slipcases could inspire me into compiling a tome of larger proportions but crammed with a mine of carefully selected, sometimes personal, factual, informative and anecdotal miscellany, seemed pertinent given that I would be dealing with just about every facet of the art world.

Following the success of my last book, *The Antiques Magpie*, it seemed obvious that I had dipped my toe into an arena that people were keen to hear more about. This compelling world, the 'illness' of collecting and the characters that populate it are like a form of antiquarian spontaneous combustion, igniting almost every day into amazing stories and snapshots of history. The idea that I could write an annual compendium by drawing on a continual torrent of startling facts about the auction world and the complex psychological machinations of collectors seemed wholly sensible to me; after all, it's a world that I'm continually in touch with. Indeed, without my diverse knowledge of art and objects it would be nigh-on impossible to divine the stories and sniff out the gossip. People were also complimentary about the personal touch that I had lent the *Magpie* in drawing on my own passion for objects and their stories but not being totally handcuffed by the art establishment. Hence the association of my name with this *Antiques Almanac*.

Never a day seems to pass when I am not regaled with yet more tales of record-breaking artworks, and considering the huge financial sums at stake it's a business that generates its fair share of drama, mystique, intrigue, elation and despondency, all encapsulated here in this eclectic collection.

I will try to abstain from prognostication and the use of language 'fitted (in plain English terms) for the apprehension of the weak' and endeavour to keep it 'serviceable for the finest wits and best capacities'★ in conveying, in the best historical tradition of almanacs, a varied and interesting account of the finest annual tales from the world of art and antiques. This is no dry collection of facts and although I felt it necessary to pepper it with a few lists and illustrations, again in the true tradition of almanacs, I'm hoping that it will prove alluring in its diversity and revelationary nature because, after all, there seems to be no limit to man's innate curiosity.

★ With apologies to Thomas Lakes, author of *The Countrey-mans Kalendar* (1627)

Thangka Lot

Money is like water, try to grab it and it flows away,
open your hands and it will move towards you.
—BUDDHA

It's no surprise that many of the most beautiful and rare objects created by man stem from his religious beliefs. I own a multi-denominational cross-section of religious artefacts ranging from glow-in-the-dark Madonnas to 10th-century bronze Buddhas, each with its own lure and personally selected irrespective of its religious connotations or my own beliefs. I recently made a trip to Sri Lanka and was captivated by the stunning UNESCO World Heritage Site of the Dambulla cave temple with its 153 statues of Buddha and over 2,000 square metres of frescoes. The complex, dating back some 2,000 years, is one of the jewels in Sri Lanka's cultural crown.

Sadly, I suspect that I will never be in the position to attain nirvana but the 18th-century thangka on my wall at home serves as a constant reminder of the possibility. So, what is a thangka?

A thangka (or tangka, or thanka, or tanka — there are several variant spellings) is an intricately painted (sometimes woven) depiction of a Buddhist deity, or a mandala — a symbolic representation of the universe — or perhaps a Buddhistic scene. Painted on textile, they are primarily instructional aids designed to explain myths and teachings, and are sometimes described as 'scroll paintings'. They exist in all Buddhist cultures including those of the Chinese, Nepalese and Tibetans. They range in size from that of a small household picture to many metres across. Large examples are used in festivals. The rise of the Eastern market in recent years has seen thangkas sell for increasingly large sums. A superb 18th-century example from a private European collection, depicting the 11th–12th-century Tibetan yogi Jetsun Milarepa, was recently sold at auction by Dreweatts & Bloomsbury for a staggering £450,000. Its size, at 1.27m by 86cm, was described as 'monumental' and the work was considered to represent the artistic height of the Karma Gardri school of Eastern Tibet known for its stylistic interpretation of Chinese influence.

Assassin's Ring

There's nothing like a good conspiracy theory to perpetuate interest in an infamous historical event. For those of us who are old enough, it's not unusual to ponder the moment when we first heard that Elvis had died or that John F. Kennedy had been assassinated. Meanwhile, the conspiracy theories continue to abound and every so often fresh items with a particular or personal relevance to those involved emerge to fuel the media frenzy. The collectors of such mementoes seem to have an insatiable appetite for all things connected with the Kennedy assassination and, despite the somewhat sad and macabre fascination of such artefacts, records are always broken when new material comes on to the market.

2013 was of course the 50th anniversary of Kennedy's death, and among the events marking the occasion was a specialist auction in Boston. Among the many Lee Harvey Oswald-related items was the window from the Texas School Book Depository from which Oswald took the fatal shot. However, the window has a particularly contentious history: at one point it was sold on eBay for $3 million but was not paid for. Conjecture about whether it is the right window may have been instrumental in it not selling during the auction. Apparently, windows in the depository were swapped and replaced and no official records were kept. This has subsequently led to a situation where various past owners of the building – as many as three – claim to own the real window. The true identity of 'the corner window' may never be determined satisfactorily. However, with irrefutable evidence from Oswald's widow, Marina Oswald Porter, the provenance of Lee Harvey's wedding ring, engraved inside with a hammer and sickle, was not in doubt. It realised $108,000 at the same auction.

Holding a Torch

No auctioneer or museum curator would be worth their salt if they didn't constantly have their eye on the possibility of cashing in on an anniversary. Whether increasing footfall in an art gallery or maximising the potential revenue from an auction lot, the historic 'tie-in' can be a major boost to an exhibition or specialist sale. Amid the controversies of the 2014 Winter Olympics at Sochi, two Parisian auctioneers in the Drouot (a building in Paris housing several auction galleries) were keen to capitalise on the timing of the event by offering rare, identical Olympic torches.

The tradition of the Olympic flame symbolises the ancient myth of Prometheus stealing fire from Zeus, the Greek god. Its use in the modern Olympic Games dates from 1936 where it was introduced by Carl Diem, the chief organiser of the infamous 1936 Olympics in Berlin. The torch relay means that for each Games, numerous examples are manufactured. For instance, 1,688 torches were made for the 1948 Games in London and 8,000 were made for the 2012 Games. Obviously, excepting some circumstances, torches are not rare; but in the case of the Winter Olympics held in Grenoble in 1968, only 33 'artisan-made' models were produced, created by the Société Technique d'Equipement et de Fourniture Industrielle. The two torches auctioned in Paris, mentioned above, were examples.

One sold by Beaussant Lefèvre realised a glowing £87,720, and another sold by Olivier Couteau-Bégarie shone out at £65,790. The record for one of these models is €192,000. In 1952, a very limited number – only 22 torches – was made for the Helsinki Olympics. These are coveted by collectors and an example was sold by Vassy-Jalenques SARL of Paris in April 2011, for €290,000.

※❦❧❀❦❧❦❀❦❧❦※

All Tied Up

Not even eternity can hold Houdini
—KATE BUSH, 'HOUDINI', *THE DREAMING* (1980)

Erik Weisz, better known as Harry Houdini, is without doubt one of the most famous magicians and escapologists in history. Born in Budapest in 1874, his family emigrated to the USA in 1878. Known as 'The Handcuff King' he began his career working in sideshows, doing card tricks with his brother. It was during this period that he started experimenting with escapology and his route to stardom was assured after a meeting in 1899 with his future manager Martin Beck.

Houdini toured Europe and America perfecting acts

such as escaping from straitjackets, being buried alive and challenging police forces to handcuff and shackle him! Houdini took great pride in the honesty of his ability and spent much time debunking frauds and cheats and pursuing people through legal channels who defamed him or inferred that he had cheated or bribed people to help him escape.

One of his most famous stunts was set up by the Daily Mirror in 1904. Their challenge was for him to break free from a special 'inescapable' cuff, a rigid version that had

taken a Birmingham locksmith, Nathaniel Hart, five years to make. If you have any knowledge of locks, the sight of the Bramah-style key would have been enough for most people to refuse the challenge, which apparently Houdini initially did, but eventually, in front of a crowd of 4,000 people at the Hippodrome in London, he undertook what he called 'one of the hardest ... tests, I have ever had'. It took Houdini over an hour to get out of the cuff, amid much conjecture and hype over whether he actually achieved it truthfully. The Mirror presented him with a solid silver set as a memento. These are now owned by collector Mike Hanzlick; the originals that were used in the challenge are today owned by the famous magician David Copperfield.

Houdini was to become one of the highest-paid performers in American vaudeville. With death-defying acts such as the 'Chinese Water Torture Cell', he captivated his audiences with ever more dangerous variations on his much-imitated tricks.

Houdini-related artefacts are much sought after. One of Harry Houdini's straitjackets sold for $46,980 at Christie's in 2011, but more recently Dreweatts & Bloomsbury have sold several interesting items including a pair of Lilly leg irons for £2,500 and an unusual pair of hand-forged cuffs made in Birmingham. Originally from the estate of the widow of Theo Hardeen, Houdini's brother, the handcuffs were the first pair of Houdini cuffs to come to auction (and there have been many) that were 'specially prepared ... to provide a sure release'. It's thought that they may have been used in his most dangerous underwater escape acts. They realised £2,300.

Houdini died of peritonitis in 1926 after suffering a ruptured appendix. He was just 52 years old.

Crystal Ball

If I had £1 for every time I've been asked the question 'what's the next big thing?' I would have retired long ago. To be frank, not even a working crystal ball would have predicted some of the recent stratospheric movements in the markets, let alone the ponderous hedging-your-bets, time-related improvement in investing in an area which over several decades sees a large increase in resale value.

So when an American gentleman by the name of Eric P. Newman started collecting coins in the 1930s, $100 dollars was a lot of money. This was precisely what he paid for a 1796 B-2 quarter-dollar, minted in the first year the US mint produced a 'quarter'. Recently sold, Newman's coin is possibly one of the finest ever to come on the market, with a near-perfect 'album toning'. Furthermore, it is one of only around 500 thought to have survived. It realised a hyper-inflationary $1.5 million at Heritage Auctions and formed part of a collection of 1,800 coins originally purchased for a total of about $7,500. The final tally for the entire collection was over $23 million!

Art Market Matters

Champagne for my real friends — real pain for my sham friends!
—FRANCIS BACON

Prior to the crash in 2008, records in the art market had been continually tumbling. The auction houses were awash with money as art was increasingly bought as a 'blue chip' commodity, soaking up the excess cash of the millionaires and billionaires trying to find a safe haven for their bulging bank balances. At the time, it seemed like the pre-crash peak was an unprecedented culmination of a one-way trip to financial ruin in a market that was fuelled by avarice, ill-gotten gains in the banking world and contempt for the real meaning of art itself. The Old Master market had remained fairly steady with the odd spectacular result — the finite supply of Rembrandts and the type of customer has always put a cap on the market. However, the modern art market periodically catches fire and prior to 2008 it was burning far more brightly than it had ever burnt before. Damien Hirst's sale on the very eve of the crash signified a peak in the idea that art is really only worth what people are prepared to pay for it, rather than having an innate value. Many critics argue that Hirst's work subsequently crashed in value because people 'got over' the delusional idea that his art is a 'gold standard' currency. Some say that Hirst's art just got bad.

I can remember 20 years ago marvelling over pictures making record prices: wow, £5 million! Even at the peak in 2007 we marvelled at a Francis Bacon making £14 million! Now look at the market post-crash: what we thought were prices never to be bettered have been reduced to ashes in the magnesium-fuelled inferno of the new capitalist onslaught. Now we see £74 million paid for a version of Edvard Munch's 'The Scream' and £89 million paid for Francis Bacon's triptych of Lucian Freud. Funny how out of so much anguish and financial heartache comes even more extraordinary excess. Where will it ever end?

Derby Day

The 1920s–40s is often regarded as the classic Hollywood era of American cinema. Actors and actresses from this golden epoch include the cream of comedy, personalities often epitomised by trademark accessories and mannerisms. None is more famous than Charlie Chaplin or Laurel and Hardy. A good friend of mine once recounted a story of the view at a Los Angeles auction. He found himself chatting to an unshaven man who was looking at a cane that had once belonged to Charlie Chaplin. After exchanging a few polite pleasantries, he realised it was Leonardo DiCaprio!

Actors who use props in the course of their career rarely rely on a single example. Various canes and bowler hats belonging to Chaplin have been offered for sale, and one such cane, used in the film *Modern Times*, was sold by Christie's in 2004 for £47,800. More recently, Bonhams sold a cane and a bowler hat (those of Chaplin's trademark *Little Tramp* character) for £37,669. I'm not sure whether Mr DiCaprio is the owner of either of these! A moustache worn by Chaplin in *The Great Dictator* was also sold in the 2004 sale for £11,950.

The bowler hat, known as a Derby hat in the USA, topped off the famous slapstick comedy duo of Laurel and Hardy. Their screen relationship blossomed from already successful careers. Stan Laurel had made over 50 films,

Charlie Chaplin with trademark cane

and Oliver Hardy over 250 films, prior to their successful partnership. The pair appeared in, or made, 107 films in total. I've filmed several items related to the duo on the *Antiques Roadshow*, a situation made more possible by their unswerving generosity in giving away countless souvenirs and autographs to their fans. A pair of Derby hats once owned by the legendary entertainers was recently sold by Bonhams in New York for £11,300.

Lapidary Legend

Loyal viewers of the *Antiques Roadshow* are very familiar with the name Fabergé, indeed, the very appearance of my colleague Geoffrey Munn often heralds the start of a fascinating story about the Russian Revolution, the demise of the Russian aristocracy and the eventual execution of Czar Nicolas II and his family. Occasioning this story are the objects that intermittently surface made by the workshop of Peter Carl Fabergé, 'Goldsmith by special appointment to the Imperial crown'. Not all Fabergé objects were made for the Russian royal family but the legendary quality and opulence of objects such as the famed Easter eggs – and the fact that several of those are still missing – continues to fuel our fascination with this fated lost dynasty.

Every so often, a lost Fabergé object surfaces to a plethora of media headlines, further intriguing tales and suggestions of untold worth. Such was the case with a staggeringly beautiful hardstone figure of Nikolai Nikolaievich Pustynnikov, the loyal personal Cossack bodyguard to Empress Alexandra Feodorovna. Czar Nicolas II commissioned the figure in 1912 as a present for his wife. It was sold by Hammer Galleries in 1934 to a Mr George Davis and stayed in the family until late 2013, when it was purchased for $5.2 million by the London jewellers and Fabergé specialist Wartski, who incidentally were Armand Hammer's main rivals for the purchase of Imperial treasures after the revolution – little wonder that Geoffrey Munn, managing director of Wartski, knows so much about the subject!

Now, you may be forgiven for thinking that this lapidary masterpiece was a fabulous, prodigious discovery and was unlikely to be trumped in the near future. Wrong! The recent announcement of the discovery of one of the missing Imperial Russian Easter eggs, not seen in public since 1902, proved to be an enormous nest egg for the American dealer who purchased it at an antiques fair for a reported $8,000. Apparently, he did so based on the weight of the scrap gold and gem content, not its aesthetic qualities. Now valued at a staggering $20 million, Wartski were once again involved in the acquisition of this rare and missing Fabergé masterpiece commissioned by Czar Alexander III in 1887. As to how many are still missing, the jury seems to be out on that one: perhaps six or seven? What we can be fairly sure of is that at some point we can expect some further big headlines.

Not on the Cheapside

I am never one to miss a good exhibition, and the historic assemblage of the Cheapside Hoard at the Museum of London between October 2013 and April 2014 was a fascinating, not-to-be-missed insight into an area of antiquity perhaps little known by many – Tudor and Jacobean jewellery. This was the first opportunity since 1914 to see a priceless collection of gemstones, jewellery, objects and ancient artefacts that were found by workmen digging in an old Cheapside cellar in 1912. There, in the remains of a wooden box, they unearthed over 500 precious objects, the like of which were known only from paintings or, incredibly, not even known at all. The high security of the exhibition reflected both this scarcity and the objects' value.

The true story or reason for their burial will never be known but it has been surmised that the hoard forms the stock-in-trade of a Jacobean goldsmith. The location on Cheapside was thought to have been the premises of a jeweller; a row of buildings in that vicinity was historically owned by the Worshipful Company of Goldsmiths in a jewellery-producing area known since medieval times. Possible reasons for the hoard's disposition have abounded: skulduggery, fire, plague, civil war. There have been various suppositions but no one can be certain.

The workmen who found the hoard quickly sold it to an infamous pawnbroker known as 'Stoney Jack', 'no questions asked'. However, the said pawnbroker, more properly known as George Fabian Lawrence, also sourced items for the London museums and was able to quickly collect the trove together and secure it for posterity. The funds for the larger part of the treasure, which went to the then new London Museum, were given by Lewis Vernon Harcourt, 1st Viscount Harcourt. Some items went to the British Museum, the Guildhall Museum and the Victoria & Albert Museum. The Museum of London exhibition was the first time the hoard had been reunited for 100 years.

Most fascinating is the fact that the hoard displays the truly international diversity of trade: emeralds from Colombia, diamonds from India and rubies from Burma. Scattered among these are Roman and Byzantine cameos and intaglios, an intricate timepiece set in a large cut emerald and, my favourite of all, a collection of toadstones. It's here that myth and reality meet in what on the face of it seems an altogether worthless collection of pebbles but is a wonderfully idiosyncratic history lesson manifested in the form of a selection of polished fossil teeth from the Lepidotes fish. Their use? Set into rings, they were invaluable aids for detecting poison and would heat up (according to myth) when put in the vicinity of a potential personal hazard. No doubt they were good sellers, as the numerous examples in the Cheapside Hoard suggests.

So, much as I moaned about being divested of much of my clothing, battling with the overly complicated lockers in the Museum of London and doing battle with the crowds of similarly irritated visitors, it was without doubt one of the best exhibitions of the year.

Severed Head

I was recently invited to dinner with a client. The meal was delightful and the banter peppered with tales of amazing objects and purchases. We retired to the drawing room for coffee and my host disappeared, returning just a few minutes later with a small, faded, leather-covered box. Embossed on the lid in gilt lettering were the words 'Relic of King Charles The Martyr'. My heart jumped. I looked at my host and flicked open the hook-shaped catch. Inside, under glass, was a lock of hair and next to it a wax seal. Printed on a small piece of paper within the lid were the words:

Relic of King Charles I
On the 11th April 1813, Sir Henry Halford,
by direction and in the presence of the Prince Regent,
superintended the opening of the coffin of Charles I,
in the vault of the George's Chapel, Windsor, for the
purpose of verifying the interment of the King.
Sir Henry removed a portion of the hair from
the right temple and also from the beard, part
of this relic he presented to its present owner, in
whose possession it has since remained – whose seal
it bears – and by whom it can be authenticated.

At that moment, a tear welled up in my eye and I felt like I was truly touching history. Value? £5,000–8,000.

The Printed Word

You cannot open a book without learning something
—CONFUCIUS

First or last? When it comes to collecting, these are the two words that more often than not define the real value of an object. The *first* book to be printed in what is now the United States of America was the Bay Psalm book of 1640. It was meant to be an accurate translation of the Hebrew Psalms into English, although it is rife with mistakes! Out of about 1,700 original copies, only eleven are thought to still exist. It was published by the Puritan leaders of the Massachusetts Bay Colony and is regarded by some as being the most important book in the nation's history. In 1947 a copy sold for a staggering $151,000 – far more at the time than even a Gutenberg Bible. The latest copy to come to sale was one of two owned by Boston's Old South Church. The price paid? A mere $14.2 million. By my reckoning that works out at about $1,420 per word.

Without Prejudice

Jane Austen is without doubt one of England's most celebrated authors. 2013 was the bicentenary of the publication of her novel *Pride and Prejudice*, an anniversary which undoubtedly was instrumental in the fervour that surrounded the rescue of a ring that had once belonged to her. One of only three pieces of jewellery known to have a personal connection to Austen, the gold and turquoise ring has an impeccable provenance and was passed through the family until it was sold by Sotheby's at auction. The ring was purchased for £152,450 by American pop star Kelly Clarkson, a fact that immediately brought it to increased attention in the media. Regarded as a significant object and of national importance, it was slapped with an export ban which allowed the nation sufficient time to raise the equivalent sale amount in order to stop it from leaving the country. The funds were raised quickly through the Jane Austen's House Museum, Chawton in Hampshire, helped by a generous anonymous donation of £100,000. The ring is now on public display.

Stovepipe

I live in Chippenham in Wiltshire and almost every day I am reminded of the great civil engineer Isambard Kingdom Brunel (1806–1859) as I pass under his imposing, multi-arched Great Western Railway viaduct that heralds the entrance into the town centre. On the same line, between Chippenham and Bath, is the Box Tunnel, a miraculous two-mile feat of Victorian engineering and one of many so-called 'impossible' projects pioneered by Brunel. Despite some failures, the legacy of his skill still provides us with infrastructure that we continue to use every day. In 2002 he was voted second in a BBC poll of the '100 Greatest Britons' and his character was central to the opening ceremony of the 2012 Olympic Games in London. A famous photographic portrait of Brunel standing in front of the launching chains of the SS *Great Eastern* portrays him smoking a cigar in his trademark stovepipe hat.

Objects associated with Brunel are highly collectable and vigorously contested at auction. Some wonderful examples have come to light over the years. A leather cigar case, bearing the embossing 'I.K.B. [Isambard Kingdom Brunel] Athenaeum Club Pall Mall' – with one cheroot still intact – sold for £26,400 at Bonhams in 2011. A cased set of wooden architects' drawing curves stamped in ink with 'I.K.B.' made £27,500 in 2012, again at Bonhams, and a

Isambard Kingdom Brunel

personal favourite of mine, sold in the same year, was a silver presentation snuff box made by the famous silver-smith Nathaniel Mills. The lid, decorated with a picture of Brunel's ship the SS *Great Britain*, the first iron-hulled, screw-powered, ocean-going steamer (now in dry dock in Bristol) is inscribed inside from the directors of the Great Western Steamship Company to Brunel. The snuff box sold for £16,000. It's thought that Brunel may once have sold it himself when the failure of the company to secure a mail contract for the great ship and her subsequently running aground near Ireland caused the company to go bankrupt.

More recently, the Brunel offerings have been more

meagre at auction but I was particularly taken with a 19th-century concertina 'peep-show' optical toy of the Thames Tunnel, the first tunnel built under a navigable river, constructed between 1825 and 1843 – both Brunel and his father, Marc Isambard Brunel, worked on the project. The toy realised a more affordable £400.

Property Bubble

Rising house prices are back in the news and it seems certain that the latest property bubble will end in tears for many overstretched buyers. Imagine then, that as the owner of a well-appointed and highly original Victorian doll's house, complete with a wonderful array of original contents, you have to decide what is the best way to sell it. Unlike France, where it's not unusual to buy a house with its chattels, it's not something that is commonplace in the UK – except with doll's houses, it seems! In this case, the owners stipulated that the contents be kept with the house and, rather unusually for an antique auction lot, the house and contents were offered for sale by Chorley's auctioneers in Gloucestershire by informal tender.

The 4ft-high doll's house was built around 1850 by a

Liverpool couple called Mr and Mrs Newton. Made for their six-year-old daughter Emma, the house was furnished with a selection of items made by the couple and additional miniature household objects purchased on foreign holidays in Germany and Switzerland – famous centres of production for every necessary scaled-down accessory! Such was the interest that the winning tender was a hefty £42,450; luckily there was no stamp duty to pay!

The £5 Raindrop

I'm not a betting man but I was intrigued by this interesting gambling story that came to light as the result of the sale of some farthing coins at Woolley and Wallis auctioneers. Apparently, a member of the Alington family from Crichel House in Dorset had a £5 wager with a friend over the speed of two raindrops running down a pane of glass. The friend lost. Given that this was in 1890, £5 was no small amount of money and the friend, rather displeased at losing the wager, paid his dues in mint farthings – 2,794 of them to be precise – all dated 1890.

£2 18s 1½d remained of the original cache when it came to auction, the coins all wrapped in their original tissue, still bright and in mint condition. They sold for £63,440. It's interesting to think what the full £5-worth might have made!

❧❧❧

Hand of Glory

In 1823, a group of leading citizens and local dignitaries led by the Rev. George Young founded the Whitby Literary and Philosophical Society. The main purpose was to set up a museum and library, which would primarily focus on locally related material including the rich fossil deposits and jet that form an important part of Whitby's working heritage. It's one of my favourite museums, mainly because it has such a quirky and eccentric collection of objects. Although the collection feels very 19th century and in some ways seems quite random, the present museum building only dates from 1931, when it was built to house an ever-increasing collection. It adjoins the municipal art gallery.

There is one very unusual exhibit, this being the main reason for my most recent visit. The object, called a 'Hand of Glory', is a rather gruesome dried severed hand, which by all accounts was taken from the body of a hanged felon. Folklore says that when furnished with a candle made of the same fat as the hand, it has the power to render people motionless, open locked doors and detect treasure. There are various methods of preparation for a Hand of Glory; one detailed in the 1722 *Secrets Merveilleux de la Magie Naturelle et Cabalistique du Petit Albert* involved various herbs, nitre and a good stint of sunshine to dry it out. Naturally, such hands are quite rare, and given Whitby's historic literary association with vampires, it attracts a rather unusual following.

Star Lot

Better a diamond with a flaw than a pebble without
—CONFUCIUS

Strange, I sometimes think, how diamonds continue to intrigue us. They are commonly occurring and yet they can command incredible prices. However, the diamonds that attract the biggest sums are not the jewellers shop window variety, they are the largest, most flawless, historic and most unusual in colour. Those which fall within the purest grading categories make up less than 2 per cent of all gems. In recent years there have been some stunningly large amounts paid.

Der Blaue Wittelsbacher or the Wittelsbach Diamond is a blue stone from the Kollur mine in India and was apparently purchased by King Philip IV of Spain in the mid-17th century. The 35.56 carat stone was mounted in the Bavarian crown for over 100 years. In 2008 it was purchased by the famous jeweller Laurence Graff for £16.4 million – at the time the highest price paid for a diamond. Contentiously for such a historic diamond, he had it recut, reducing its weight by over 4 carats. However, this significantly improved its clarity and grading. The current value is thought to be around $80–100 million.

Recent higher achievers have included the 14.23 carat Perfect Pink sold for £14.8 million in 2010; the 12 carat Martian Pink sold in 2012 for £11.1 million; the 76.45 carat Archduke Joseph, sold in the same year for £13.5 million; in 2013, the 101.73 carat Winston Legacy sold for £17.5 million, the 14.82 carat vivid orange diamond known as The Orange sold for £22.3 million, and the 34.65 carat Princie Diamond sold for £24.7 million – and all this without mentioning the record holder since 2010, the 23.88 Graff Pink at £28.8 million. However, all of this seemed like pocket money when the flawless 59.60 carat Pink Star was sold by Sotheby's for £51.7 million, only to glimmer in the record books for a short period when it transpired that the buyer(s) had defaulted and the diamond was not paid for. Ever since, speculation has been rife as to why this happened. The default has even been linked to human rights issues. Perhaps we will never know the truth ...

Holey Grail

It's an expression that's continually used in the world of antiques and collectables: the 'Holy Grail' – e.g. 'of the camera world'. I've been guilty of using it myself, but sometimes, although it's rather clichéd, it seems difficult to express the rarity of an object in any other way. Funny, I thought, when reading a recent edition of the *Antiques Trade Gazette* I happened to see the headline 'Holey Grail of Australian Coins takes £160,000'. So what's with the pun?

The first coins to be struck in Australia were known as the 'Colonial Dump' and the 'New South Wales Holey Dollar'. They were struck in 1813. Prior to this the economy had been unstable and the people had been using rum as currency – which was not a particularly stable way of evolving a burgeoning new economy. In an attempt to turn things around, the governor, Lachlan Macquarie, imported 40,000 Spanish silver dollars, which were re-struck with a hole in the centre and an inner legend 'New South Wales 1813'. This was given a face value of five shillings. The piece that was punched out of the centre was called the 'Colonial Dump' and again marked 'New South Wales, 1813' with a crown in the centre on one side, the obverse marked with the value: fifteen pence. Quite an innovative idea! These coins were used up until 1829 when the sterling standard was reintroduced. Most were then recalled and melted down. However some did survive and it's thought that around 300 Holey Dollars and 800 Colonial Dumps escaped the melt when they were shipped off to London as bullion. The combination of such an interesting history and obvious rarity makes these highly sought after – hence the £160,000 paid for the 'Holey Grail' of Australian coins.

New South Wales Holey Dollar and Colonial Dump

Sleepers

Without wishing to sound too cynical, viewing auctions usually revolves around trying to divine something that no one else has spotted or deciphered, *then* trying to keep your nerve until the day of the sale while hoping to carry it off for as little money as possible. It doesn't matter whether you are buying for profit or to complete your collection, the thrill of the chase and the chance of a bargain is enough for us to continually pit our wits against the people who are meant to know better. Of course, people can't know it all, and it's an age-old phenomenon that keeps people coming back to shops where they once had a bargain or auction houses where goods are underestimated or badly catalogued. Interestingly, from my personal experience, it's rare to 'steal' an object because the internet advertises things so well. Poor cataloguing and low starting prices often serve to fuel the pre-sale hysteria and the object usually goes to even greater heights than it may have done if it weren't lurking in a box hidden under a table.

Here are a few 'sleepers' that have recently come to light:

1. Estimated at £200–300 in Charterhouse auctions in Sherborne, Dorset, a set of four Chinese famille rose wooden-framed porcelain panels by an artist known as one of The Eight Friends of Zhushan, key Republican decorators who revived the ceramics industry after the Qing dynasty fell (the last emperor abdicated in 1912), made £420,000.
2. A Louis XV dish by the Vincennes factory, made for the king as part of a large service between 1753 and 1755 at the cost of 87,272 livres and estimated at just £70–90 by Wellers of Guildford, made £70,000 hammer price.

Catalogued as Sèvres, many people could have been for-given for not spotting it, but it still made its money!

3. My wife spotted a small 'blue and white mug' in the local auction and identified it as Lowestoft. At £30–40 the estimate was a bit on the low side: she bid it to £1,400 and didn't get it!

4. J.S. Auctions near Banbury were no doubt surprised when a jade 'tablet' recently made an eye-watering £520,000 (including commission). With no estimate and a very brief catalogue description the piece had appar-ently been consigned from a private estate in Oxford. The jade carried an inscription which, translated, read:

> This very beautiful and flawless Hetian jade, look-ing like ointment, was made into an axe pendant carved in an archaic way with complicated deco-rations, but has been recently worked over by philistine craftsmen to make it worth more but actually damaged its origin. It will be the bad fate a jade is discarded, so I write my words on it.

On the piece was the seal of the Emperor Qianlong himself and these, purporting to be his words, made this a highly sought object with the Chinese market – hence the price. Another jade of two sages from the same source made £78,000.

5. I've seen this happen on more than one occasion and it's why I always look carefully at large pairs of old binoculars. Favourite among collectors are the Zeiss Kriegsmarine 'bins' issued to German U-boat commanders. They are optically superb with a large field of vision and are pretty rare so it's not surprising they slip by the odd auction house cataloguer. Mitchells auctioneers in Cumbria had such a pair turn up from a local house clearance and as interest garnered on a £30–40 estimate, the auctioneers soon realised something had slipped through. A revised estimate of £800–1,200 seemed more appropriate and they sold for £2,900. I once sold a pair for £3,300 and found another pair on the *Antiques Roadshow* – so they do surface occasionally (no pun intended).

6. Collecting photographs in albums was a popular pastime in the Victorian period. I've been on many house valuations and found large leather-bound tomes variously filled with Grand Tour pictures of famous sculptures from the Vatican, images of the pyramids and snapshots of the Crystal Palace Exhibition. Most of these are commercially produced 'souvenir' photographs, although that's not to say they aren't potentially valuable.

   Part of the skill with these albums is spotting what is rare and sought after. Often that's to do with historical context and subject, or possibly the original photographer – or a mixture of all these factors. You have to be careful. Shapes Auctioneers in Edinburgh realised this when an album from a house clearance, mainly full of Scottish scenes and priced at £40–60, suddenly gained attention. The album also contained around 40 images from the American Civil War, one specifically showing a black American surrendering to some Union soldiers. This was undoubtedly a staged photograph: photographic techniques of the period did not allow quick snapshots to be taken. However, the £1,700 paid on the hammer was probably still a bargain considering the subject matter and I can't help thinking that once these get to the USA the value will be considerably higher!

Past Picassos

The people who make art their
business are mostly imposters
—PABLO PICASSO

I'm a keen amateur photographer and although I fancy myself as a bit of a Man Ray I have to bow to the skill of other great photographers when it comes to selecting things to put on the walls. One of my favourites is a black and white portrait print of Pablo Picasso by Lee Miller (1907–1977), the American photographer, war correspondent and model who famously posed in Hitler's bath. The connection here is really Picasso; they were lovers and the photograph is cloaked with meaning. It has always intrigued me.

Born in Spain in 1881, Picasso is regarded as one of the most important artists of the 20th century and the founding father of the Cubist movement. The art market, despite the apparent economic problems in the world, seems to know no limits and Picasso's work continues to attract some of the highest prices. His work 'Nude, Green Leaves and Bust' (1932) was sold by Christie's in 2010 for a world-record price for a Picasso of £62,310,500. It will undoubtedly be surpassed in time: these records rarely seem to hold for long. In the meantime, here are the top ten Picasso prices for the last year.

Top 10 prices for Picasso 2013–14

Femme Assise près d'une Fenêtre (1932)
Oil on canvas
Sold for £25,500,000, Sotheby's, London

Tête de Femme (1935)
Oil on canvas
Sold for £22,180,400, Sotheby's, New York

Mousquetaire à la Pipe (1969)
Oil on canvas
Sold for £17,182,000, Sotheby's, New York

Claude et Paloma (1950)
Oil on canvas
Sold for £15,702,500, Christie's, New York

Femme au Béret Orange et au col de Fourrure
(*Marie-Thérèse*) (1937)
Oil on canvas
Sold for £6,711,040, Christie's, New York

Nu Accroupi (1960)
Oil on canvas
Sold for £6,500,000, Christie's, London

Buste d'Homme (1969)
Oil on canvas
Sold for £5,462,950, Sotheby's, New York

Femme Assise dans un Fauteuil (1960)
Oil on canvas
Sold for £5,400,000, Christie's, London

Mandoline et Portée de Musique (1923)
Oil, sand on canvas
Sold for £5,218,830, Christie's, New York

Femme Assise en Costume Rouge sur Fond Bleu (1953)
Oil on panel
Sold for £4,832,250, Christie's, New York

Axe Hero

I'm a keen guitarist and the owner of several interesting examples. I'm always fascinated by instruments that have been played and owned by famous musicians, the craftsmanship and the history surrounding them. Over my years on the *Antiques Roadshow* I've been lucky enough to film Marc Bolan (of T. Rex fame)'s Gibson Flying V; I've strummed Joe Strummer (of the Clash)'s beautiful Gibson ES; I've mused over rare American pre-war jazz guitars such as an arch-top Slingerland May-Bell Nite Hawk; and I've taken my plectrum to numerous Hofners, Fenders and Rickenbackers, all to appreciative crowds who seem to like a tune on the day!

However, a very rare guitar recently came up for sale at Gardiner Houlgate near Bath. This well-catalogued example of a mid-17th-century 'five course' Baroque guitar, made by Matteo Sellas of Venice, had an impeccable provenance. The auction house has an increasing reputation for its guitar sales and in this instance the instrument attracted plenty of international interest. The National Music museum in Dakota – probably the best museum in the world for instruments – has two of these guitars in its collection; the Metropolitan Museum of Art in New York has one. Gardiner Houlgate's example made £48,000 plus commission of 18 per cent. I live in hope of seeing one on the *Roadshow*!

Eye Eye

Art is a lie that makes us realise the truth
—PABLO PICASSO

Few can deny the iconic status of the surrealist artist Salvador Dalí. Born in 1904 in Figueres in the Catalan region of Spain, his life was characterised by an eccentric flamboyance that at times polarised the art world. His skill and imagination enabled him to work in just about every medium: he was an accomplished painter, film maker and ceramicist, drawing inspiration from just about every other known movement and art form ranging from the Renaissance to the Cubists. Iconic works such as The Persistence of Memory, Lobster Telephone, and the

Mae West Lips Sofa, have come to symbolise and denote major themes throughout Dalí's work, such as time, religion and sexuality. His love of the avant-garde and the downright bizarre, and his controversial political views, never failed to fuel his reputation as a living embodiment of his art, a personification of surrealism – a movement, in fact, that he was expelled from in 1934. Naturally, Dalí's response was robust: 'I myself am surrealism'. Few would disagree.

In the 1940s Dalí had begun to collaborate with the Argentinian-born jeweller Carlos Alemany of New York. Between 1941 and 1970 Alemany translated a series of designs by Dalí into actual jewellery, which forms a collection now housed in a separate annex of the Dalí Museum in Figueres. Among these designs was a distinctively themed piece known as The Eye of Time (*El Ojo Del Tiempo*); Dalí designed this brooch for his wife Gala in 1949. The brooch is in the form of an eye, comprising a blue enamelled timepiece mounted as the iris and pupil – signed 'Dalí' on the dial – within diamond-set eyelids. A cabochon ruby forms the caruncle; below is a diamond-encrusted teardrop. It is without doubt one of his most iconic jewellery designs. Alemany produced a very limited number of Dalí's designs and they rarely appear for sale. When a good example of *El Ojo Del Tiempo* recently surfaced at Dreweatts auctioneers, the impeccable Italian family provenance and its original box helped it surpass an estimate of £8,000–12,000 to sell for a far more eye-watering hammer price of £75,000.

Dresser Designs

Dr Christopher Dresser (1834–1904), a Scot by birth, is one of the most important designers of the 19th century. As a 'hungry for knowledge' youngster there were several seminal designers that fascinated me in my early formative years – and still do. There was no internet then, so I relied upon reading books, visiting houses and museums and talking to people who knew far more than I did. This was how I learnt. Foremost on the list was William Burges, the great architect and designer; also A.W.N. Pugin and Archibald Knox – but Dresser somehow seemed more enigmatic, more challenging and also more likely to yield tangible objects from his vast catalogue of designs, a valuable incentive as I searched the car boot fairs and auctions for missing gems.

Dresser's design ethic was revolutionary and highly influential among his peers. He saw a burgeoning Victorian middle class that wanted and needed stylish useable objects that could be manufactured on a relatively large scale but at affordable prices. The range of designs that he produced for companies such as Minton and Wedgwood ranged from decorative ceramics to tableware, textiles, metalwork, wallpaper and glassware. He was the Philippe Starck of the Victorian era, applying industrial principles and methods of production to produce eminently useful and often challenging objects. He drew his varied influences from exotic climes such as South America and Japan but instilled modernist and sometimes futuristic feeling into some of his pieces, particularly the metalwork.

Dresser's inestimable reputation in the history of design lay strangely dormant for some decades but he is now valued for his challenging approach to many aspects of design and production. For this reason, his objects are highly sought after, particularly by museums. Hunting for Dresser items requires a fairly diverse remit. His ornamentation is varied but trademark characteristics on metalwork such as electroplated cruet sets and toast racks include T-bar handles and spherical joints, whereas ceramic designs range from pure aesthetic movement to Peruvian-style drip-glazed pieces. One of the conundrums with Dresser is that his legacy is not fully documented, which means that some designs are only attributed to him.

It's during the 1870s that we see some of his most enduring designs. Values remain fairly constant for these: letter racks and toast racks tend to sell for around

£400 depending on the model; a cruet will cost a similar amount. However, rare designs made during his successful collaborations with Hukin & Heath of Birmingham, James Dixon & Sons of Sheffield and Elkington & Co. can be far higher. Recent results compounded this with a possibly unique Elkington plated teapot sold by Woolley & Wallis auctioneers for £15,000! Reeman Dansie auctioneers also sold a very futurist prototype for £19,000 – a design that was thought too 'modern' to put into production. Another recent lucky purchase was a three-legged tureen. It was clearly marked 'Dr C Dresser 2189', but had never been seen in this variation before. It was purchased for £5 at a car boot sale and sold by Wellers Auctioneers for £1,800!

Christopher Dresser is undoubtedly one of the most innovative designers of the 19th century. From the simple understated functionality of a toast rack to the lush oriental Japonaiserie of his textiles, he deserves his place as a giant in British design history.

Face to Face

A portrait is a painting with something
wrong with the mouth
—JOHN SINGER SARGENT

Portraiture is a term generally applied to the artistic representation of a person. It's an art form spanning several millennia and it's a key way of us coming face to face with our ancestors, depicted in a tangible, albeit sometimes stylised way. Before the advent of photography it was the most accurate record of the human face. Portraits can be executed in several mediums, be it sculpture, watercolour, lithography or oil painting, the latter most often referred to as 'portrait painting'. The walls of my house are littered with such artworks: 17th-century gentlemen rub shoulders with prim ladies and stately looking personalities – my instant ancestors, as I like to call them.

Identifying the sitters can often be difficult. Unless there is a label or a name associated with the person portrayed, identities are often lost to history and stern Victorian couples commonly find themselves sitting on a shelf at auction bearing the brunt of the usual criticisms – 'Isn't she miserable-looking?' or 'He's got a kind face'. These are the savvy decorator's portable wallpaper, the chimney-breast dignitaries that commonly abound in the salerooms and they usually constitute very good value. However, by no means all come unidentified and a wonderful bonus of my line of work is that I frequently get to rub noses with some pretty important personalities – portraits, that is!

One gentleman that immediately springs to mind is the Flemish Baroque artist Sir Anthony Van Dyke, favourite court portraitist of Charles I. The artist's last self-portrait, painted shortly before he died in 1641, was the subject of a temporary export ban and campaign to raise £12.5 million to save the picture for the nation. The purchaser, my colleague Philip Mould, portraiture specialist and expert on the *Antiques Roadshow*, had secured the historic portrait in 2008 for a then-auction record for a Van Dyke of £8.3 million and I was lucky enough to visit him at Philip's gallery on several occasions. When Philip then sold him to an American collector, an export ban came into force and the fundraising began! Despite some controversy over the importance of the picture and its value, a successful campaign resulted in public donations of £1.4 million and major contributions from the Art Fund and National Portrait Gallery. The price was also dropped to £10 million and now this beautifully fluid and distinctively stylish self-portrait of the great master will join the ranks of other important portraits in the national collection. Meanwhile, I'm wondering who I will get to rub noses with next!

Me Old China

If you were asked to make a connection between William Copeland and Thomas Garrett (the famous Georgian ceramicists), two inns in Stoke-on-Trent and a pile of bones left over from a celebratory dinner, you would be unlikely to associate them all with a unique pair of cabinet cups that recently sold for £32,000. However, if you know anything about the ingredients of china, or more precisely bone china, you would quickly be able to see that the skeletal remains of the dinners at the Talbot and Wheatsheaf Inns – where the two gentlemen signed their famous partnership of 1834 (forming Copeland & Garrett) – were intrinsic to the make-up of the two unusually designed cabinet cups.

Bone china was a brilliant invention and revolutionised the British ceramics industry. It became the perfect substitute for the hard-paste porcelain originally invented by the Chinese. Its constituents are bone ash, kaolin and feldspathic material, i.e. mineral or feldspar. Originally perfected by Josiah Spode (the Elder) between 1788 and 1793, this popular type of soft-paste porcelain became the mainstay of many major British factories in the Stoke-on-Trent area. On the occasion of the two men joining forces and signing their historic agreement, the ox bones left over from the dinners were used in the manufacture of these particular cabinet cups and two additional punch bowls. The cups and bowls were sold at the Trelissick House sale in Cornwall and formed part of the Copeland Collection of Spode. Bonhams auction specialist and *Antiques Roadshow* expert Henry Sandon said, 'This is as important a piece of factory history as you could get.' At £32,000, the buyer obviously thought so too.

Baaa-ber

How long do think it would take to shear 321 merino sheep? In 1893 a gentleman by the name of Jackie Howe managed the feat in seven hours and forty minutes – with hand shears! This record has never been broken. Dubbed the 'Bradman of the boards' for his remarkable speed, he had already broken the record for mechanical shearing the previous year, winning himself two gold medals. These were sold in 2008 by Sotheby's in Australia for Aus$360,000.

More recently, a pair of mechanical shears presented to Howe in 1893 by the Wolseley Sheep Shearing Machine Company, were offered for sale at Sotheby's Melbourne Rooms. The buyers were the National Museum of Australia and, including the buyer's commission of 22 per cent,

Mr Howe's reputation as the fastest sheep-shearer in history pushed the lot up to just under £30,000!

Who Pays the Ferryman?

According to Greek mythology, Charon is the ferryman of Hades. It was his job to take the souls of the dead across the rivers Styx and Acheron and the customary payment would be a coin placed in or on the mouth of the dead person – the ferryman's fare, so to speak. Strangely enough, it seems the custom eventually made its way to China but rather than using actual coins, the Chinese used faux coins made of very thin gold but based on the familiar form of Chinese bronze coins used for over 2,000 years – commonly known as 'cash' – which feature a square hole in the centre. Incidentally, these are so common and of such little value that they were often used to weigh down curtain hems!

As gold was historically scarce in China it was used very sparingly in most applications. The faux coins, which are very rare, have gold weights of as little as a tenth of a gram. One such example dating from the Tang Dynasty (AD618–907) was recently sold in a sale in Hong Kong for £195, which, if you don't mind owning something that's been in a dead person's mouth, seems like fairly good value to me!

Not Allum's Almanac

Almanacs are historically small, much smaller than this tome. Had this been typical 'almanac' size I wouldn't have laboured for six months – but then again you probably wouldn't have found it fulsome enough to buy either! Almanacs are, by the nature of the time-sensitive content, works generally to be discarded, although I hope that you will keep mine for a while before relegating it to the charity shop!

The rarest examples date from the very origins of the genre and one such gem surfaced at a rare manuscripts sale at Christie's King Street. Measuring just 13cm by 4cm, this scarce folding almanac comprising seven leaves folded into three sections fits neatly into an embroidered velvet and silk purse which could be hung on a belt. This indicates its use as a portable source of information with calendrical, medical and astrological material all included.

Thought to be one of no more than 30 such examples in existence, it dates from *c.*1415–20. Most are in collections and ten are held by the British Library. The highlight of this particular example is its illuminated image of Zodiac man and the format follows John Somer's *Kalendar ad meridiem Oxonie* of 1386, a work prepared under the patronage of Joan of Kent, Princess of Wales and mother of Richard II. It also has the added kudos of having once belonged to Dame Edith Sitwell. Fortuitously, the new custodians are the Wellcome Library which makes it available for further study. What value such a rare medieval almanac? It was sold on the day for £100,000.

Street Life

If you have an idea what 'market stalls' means in cockney rhyming slang then you might find Thomson and Smith's photographic *Street Life of London* rather interesting. Originally issued in twelve monthly parts spanning 1877–78, it was subsequently published in book form and was a pioneering pictorial Victorian work that socially documented the streets of London. Each volume contains 26 Woodbury types, a clever printing process that accurately reproduced the tonal quality of photographs and was developed by Walter B. Woodbury in 1864. The quality of the

Image from *Street Life of London*

prints is extremely good and the reproductions are imbued with a tonality and depth that beautifully captures the true feel of the Victorian streets. Auctioneers Dominic Winter were able to offer an example for sale recently. It had several problems including old water stains; it was also missing the preface and a page of contents but despite this it made a record £10,500.

✿

Base Metal

Mention the word 'shipwreck' and visions of lost Spanish gold or Second World War treasure ships stacked with ingots of precious metal intended to pay off foreign armies immediately spring to mind. However, this notion of value has changed over the years and despite the important archaeological value of shipwrecks, a multi-million pound business has evolved over the past few decades which centres on the commercial exploration and salvage of material from shipwrecks. The operations of these companies are sometimes contentious and they are often dubbed as opportunist treasure hunters. Famous cargoes that essentially started to turn the tide of this perception included the huge quantities of Chinese porcelain discovered on the VOC (Dutch East India Company) ship the *Geldermalsen*, known as the 'Nanking Cargo'. The ship sank on a reef in the South China Sea in 1752 along with her cargo of porcelain, tea, silk and lacquer wares. Discovered by explorer and salvor Mike Hatcher, this collection – mainly the porcelain – was sold by Christie's in 1986 and created a media frenzy. Hatcher later repeated this success in 1999 with the discovery of the *Tek Sing*, a wreck which yielded 360,000 pieces of precious porcelain cargo.

Despite the commercial implications it has become clear that the word 'treasure' is not necessarily associated with opportunists pillaging wrecks for precious metal, although such people are still around; instead, specialist private companies such as the famous Odyssey Marine Exploration organisation invest large amounts of money in technology, professional personnel and research to track down material that would not ordinarily see the light of day. In doing so they now have to be rigorous in their archaeological endeavours and produce justifiable solutions for proceeding with recoveries. Of course, large quantities of gold bullion are very helpful but their rewards are usually heavily negotiated with governments and/or owners of material. A quick visit to their website highlights a wealth of archaeological discoveries, expert papers which qualify their professionalism, and fascinating finds ranging from the most humble artefacts to the most precious objects. The discoveries include myriad hitherto unknown locations of lost historic ships and submarines; but this does not exclude them from controversy, as was highlighted by the discovery of HMS *Victory*, the predecessor of Nelson's flagship, in 2008. The ship, which sank in the English Channel in

1744 with the loss of Admiral Sir John Balchen, 1,000 hands and a reputed £600 million worth of bronze cannon and gold, created a storm when the organisation was accused of exploring it without a licence and desecrating a maritime grave. Such are the intricacies of juggling a myriad of complicated issues with such historic marine sites.

More humble was the discovery of a wreck in 2011 off the coast of the Dominican Republic by the private company Anchor Research (part of Global Marine Exploration). The 16th-century ship was near to the island of Hispaniola and full of trade goods including a particularly large quantity of rare pewter comprising approximately 1,200 pieces. Now known as the 'pewter wreck', it's thought that the ship was carrying the new Spanish Ambassador to the island in the 1540s. He was the sole survivor of the wreck. What is certain is that the discovery has changed many precepts about pewter and its manufacture. It's the single largest collection of pewter ever recovered from a wrecked ship and possibly one of the earliest consignments of pewter to (almost) reach the New World. What is even more interesting is that among the many different makers, indicated by their touch marks on the pieces, 30 per cent of the haul was by eminent London maker Sir Thomas Curtis, once Lord Mayor of London (1557) and the same maker whose wares were found on the *Mary Rose*. The pewter was unused when it went down, so these examples of porringers, salt cellars, broad-bordered chargers, etc. are in some cases almost like new – devoid of the scratches of everyday use. Seventy-five per cent of the cargo belongs to the Dominican Republic and 25 per cent to the salvage company, who recently sold their portion with specialist period auctioneers Wilkinson's of Doncaster. The final hammer price was a respectable £250,000.

Monster Price

Everyone loves to claim a record. Sometimes, in order to do so it seems that you have to jiggle the criteria a little. So it was recently when an American auction house realised the highest-ever price for a movie poster – of sorts. Movie posters, of course, come in various shapes and sizes but one particular variety is the 'insert movie poster', a smaller poster designed to fit in the glass display case outside the cinema. They roughly measure around 35cm by 91cm.

Heritage Auctions of Dallas, well known for their spectacular movie-related sales, recently offered an original 1931 'insert' poster for *Frankenstein* starring Boris Karloff. The owner had apparently purchased the poster in a shop in Ottawa, Illinois in the late 1960s and recalled paying a few dollars for it. The existing record for such a poster type had already been set by Heritage Auctions the previous year at $160,000 for a 1942 insert of *Casablanca*. The *Frankenstein* insert smashed that record by taking a hammer price of $220,000 (around £151,000). I'm sure it will be beaten in next year's instalment of *Allum's Antiques Almanac*.

Solid Gold

It's probably a little known fact that there were only two Olympic Games where the medals were made of solid gold. One was the 1908 event held in London, the other in Stockholm in 1912. Various associated auctions took place in the year of the last London Olympics and several medals were offered from the 1908 games, including the gold awarded to Raymond Etherington-Smith, captain of the Leander Club eight which represented Great Britain at rowing. It realised £17,500. (Incidentally, the Belgian crew who were considered their main opposition sank during the race, not that that should diminish the achievement of Etherington-Smith and his team.) Another gold was recently offered by Fellows auctioneers from the same eight. However, although engraved around the border

'Eight oared race' it seems unclear who the recipient was. Nonetheless, and perhaps this is indicative of selling things on an important anniversary or event, it made a sturdy but less spectacular splash than the captain's medal at £7,500.

Stamp of Disapproval

Museum dispersals and 'sell-offs' are often very contentious. We all know that the material on display in the country's galleries and museum collections is like the tip of an iceberg. Under the sparkling floors of the exhibition space lie vaults and cellars full of unseen treasures and humdrum items. Secret warehouses heated to 21°C, are stuffed full of incredible material and I've been in some staggeringly surreal museum depositories over the years. Of course, some objects see the light of day in special exhibitions and retrospectives and no one in their right mind would expect all our museums to be able to display all that they hold. However, the problems start to arise when they decide to dispose of material to perhaps raise funds for work such as building repairs. Ethically, public museums adhere to a code of conduct monitored by The Museums Association and material within those museums often comes with strict caveats, having been donated by benefactors who stipulated that it was not to be sold on, or else plainly belonging to the public under the guardianship of elected bodies and officials.

Croydon Council recently caused a certain amount of outrage by announcing that it would sell 24 pieces of its important Chinese ceramics collection in order to raise funds for redeveloping Fairfield Halls, a major concert venue. The pieces formed part of the Riesco collection purchased from a Croydon businessman in 1959. Immediately, various bodies were up in arms over the proposed sale and The Museums Association accused the council of 'asset stripping' its collection and a 'breach of the code of ethics'. It was hoped that the council would be taken to court to stop them selling the items but apparently campaigners could not raise enough money to pay the legal fees. The Museums Association also proposed that Arts Council England should 'strip Croydon Council of their status of an accredited museum authority'. Despite the opposition, the council went ahead to sell seventeen pieces with Sotheby's in Hong Kong for £8 million. So much for ethics!

Another highly contentious sell-off was the recent dispersal of 'duplicates' from the British Postal Museum & Archive (BPMA). Although approved by the Museums Association Ethics Committee, the sale was described by Gavin Littaur, a prominent postal historian and composer, as a 'fire sale'. He also strongly contested the idea that the rare pieces were all duplicates and claimed that the 191 lots were not lotted in a way that was appropriate to smaller buyers and collectors. The material on offer was not part of the BPMA's accessioned collections but Littaur's warnings that the 'ill-conceived' sale held by Sotheby's would mainly benefit the stamp dealers Stanley Gibbons and their investment portfolio largely fell on deaf ears. Interestingly enough, just prior, Stanley Gibbons announced that they would not be attending the sale, perhaps realising the contentious nature of a mass 'buy-up'. Otherwise, though, Mr Littaur's predictions were proved to be completely correct and only 29 of the 191 lots found buyers, raising a paltry £334,100 on the predicted £5.75 million estimate. All in all a prime example of a national museum collection disposal handled very poorly. Mr Littaur further argued that 'the archive has now been exposed in an inappropriate manner, damaging the reputations of those involved' and leaving the museum in a situation where it was forced to consider 'after-sales at a knockdown price'. No doubt questions have been asked at all levels about the handling of the sale, and the security of nationally important material within collections will certainly continue to be an issue where institutions see disposal as a potential route to financial security and funding.

Women's Rights

The history of women's rights and the freedom to vote is a story of hard-nosed resolve, determination to fight a male-dominated society that was ever reluctant to let go of its grip; a story of heroissm, radicalism and women united in a common cause to rightly have a say in society. New Zealand was the first self-governing country to give women the vote, doing so for all over the age of 21 in 1893. Britain lagged behind and the largely middle-class sector that constituted most women who supported the movement was indicative of the repressive social and economic system that they found themselves in. Material associated with the history of female emancipation is consequently highly collectable.

Members of the cause and particularly the Women's Social and Political Union (WSPU) were generally called suffragettes and their house magazine *Votes for Women* acted as their mouthpiece. The August 1908 edition describes 'the latest novelty in the Union colours [purple, white and green] – a special belt and buckle, which is being sold at half a crown each'. These are extremely rare and the buckle, cast with a rendition of a cartoon by David Wilson called 'The Haunted House', depicts a female ghost hovering over the Houses of Parliament with a ballot box. It was sold, together with a WSPU sash, by Clevedon

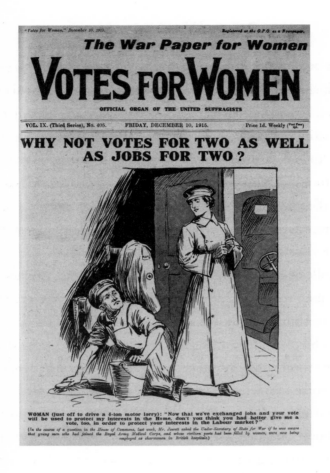

Salerooms and realised £3,400. The buyer said he had been collecting suffragette items for 50 years and had never seen one!

Lest We Forget

As we commemorate the 100-year anniversary of the Great War we find ourselves immersed in a plethora of material on the television and in the media. Revisiting the raw horror and emotive evidence that surrounds the conflict has caused many to look at newly available archival film, photographs and stories, the involvement of our families and, in my business, the tangible artefacts that are often related to the tales of heroic acts and all too often the poignant, tragic results of mass destruction.

Collecting First World War material is big business. That may sound like an awful summation but collectors acquire things for different reasons. In the aftermath of such a huge conflict, a 'machine-age' industrial war where cavalry was finally proved obsolete and the tank was born, the nature of society was changed forever. With a whole generation almost wiped out, the idea that such a war could never happen again still resounds in history – a lesson not learnt, as the horror of the Second World War soon enough proved. However, the sheer quantity of material that was generated by the scale of the war compels our museums to acquire everything from the humble missives written from the trenches to the highest award for valour in the face of the enemy – the Victoria Cross. There are the relic collectors, the people who still scour the battlefields looking for the rusty helmets, the mangled horseshoes and the cap badges. There are the collectors of 'trench art': souvenirs fashioned from the waste of war, embossed shell cases and cigarette lighters fashioned from bullets. There are the collectors of ephemera: the posters, the postcards, the letters and the photographs. And there are the medal collectors. These are just a few of the areas that motivate people to accumulate the objects of the Great War. From a few pounds to several million (for a Victoria Cross) there's something for every pocket.

In the general stunned outpouring of post-war grief, an artistic and cultural legacy also evolved in the form of memorial sculpture and commemorative artworks. Among the most famous commissioned memorials are the Cenotaph in Whitehall and the Royal Artillery Memorial on Hyde Park Corner, the latter designed by Charles Jagger and Lionel Pearson. Although such memorials served as central focuses of commemoration in the capital, cities, towns and villages all over the country commissioned their own commemorative sculptures and monuments. Sometimes, different artists would tender for possible commissions; not all were successful. The sheer power of much of the sculptural pieces of this period often lends such work an innate ability to convey the sheer horror, gallantry or even resignation of the combatants. A more recent tribute to the great slaughter of the war commemorates the millions of animals that have died in conflict; this is the Animals in War Memorial, on the edge of Hyde Park in London, by David Backhouse. It was unveiled in 2004 and, like all memorials, would have started life as a maquette or reduced version of the full-size monument. Occasionally, such versions come to the market and Duke's Auctioneers of Dorchester recently sold a bronze by the artist Robert Lindsey Clark. The piece is called 'The Broken Limber' and is a highly evocative and animated depiction of two horses struggling to pull a broken gun limber from the mud with a soldier atop. It was originally intended as a design for a full-size version in the town of Cheltenham but this was never executed. The small version was shown at the Royal Academy in 1924 and later sold to an army captain who served in the Great War. Regarded by many as one of Clark's greatest works, at the Duke's auction it came with original papers and realised £48,000, plus 20 per cent commission.

Plan Ahead

Several years ago in Swindon I filmed a fascinating collection of architectural plans for the *Antiques Roadshow*. They had come from a local practice, having been consigned to the skip but rescued by a local man. All the plans dated from the 1920s and 30s and I was immediately impressed by the artistic nature of the designs. Not only were they stylistically very indicative of the period but they instantly struck me as being part of a larger historical record of the town as it had evolved from its Saxon roots into one of the pre-eminent centres of Isambard Kingdom Brunel's Great Western Railway repair and production.

I asked the owner if he had made any exploratory reconnoitres around the town to see how many of the buildings and houses were still in existence, which he had. Surprisingly, an attempt to sell the original plans to the contemporary owners of one magnificent house had failed miserably, an opportunity I would have eagerly jumped at had I been in the same situation.

Not so the plans for Perrycroft, a wonderful Arts and Crafts house near Malvern designed by the famous Charles Francis Annesley Voysey (1857–1941). Built for John William Wilson, a railway magnate and politician, as his 'summer house', it is a gem of Arts and Crafts design. Restored in recent years, the owners were lucky enough to be able to buy a number of original plans and pieces of ephemera at Stroud Auction Rooms after a lady attending a valuation day arrived with a collection of material relating to the house. Not knowing its potential interest she had considered taking it to the dump but luckily had decided to have it appraised. The main elevation, executed by Voysey himself, was returned to its rightful place at Perrycroft for a sturdy bid of £9,800.

⁕⁂⁕

Queen Anne's Statute

My house came with a medieval title. It's known as a Burgage House, which makes me a Burgess or Freeman. These days, there are few actual benefits to this, although I am by all accounts able to ride my horse over the town bridge and graze my sheep on various pieces of land.

The charter that enshrined this title was bestowed upon the Burgesses of Chippenham by Queen Mary in 1554 and the actual charter resides in the local museum. The huge vellum document, resplendent with a naïve portrait of Queen Mary, has a large wax seal. The curator was recently kind enough to let me view it and I felt quite emotional as I touched this local piece of history (albeit with gloves on!). So as I pass out of my front door under the initialled date plaque 'G.L. 1717' – the initials being those of the vicar Gilbertius Lake who once lived in my house; it was later owned in 1826 by the MP for Chippenham E.F. Maitland, and later still by a Boer War Captain, Herbert Thomas de Carteret Hobbs of the 62nd Foot, who sadly was killed in action in 1900 – I can but wonder over the fact that they were all Burgesses too, and perhaps they were all interested enough to gaze upon the same charter?

Gatekeeper

Architectural antiques are immensely popular as interior design statements and over the years an increasing number of designers have promoted the use of outsize, surreal and juxtaposed pieces. One such dealer is LASSCO (The London Architectural Salvage and Supply Company), perhaps one of the best-known architectural antiques suppliers in the country. Salvage fairs have also become popular attractions as people collect period material for renovations and for decorative purposes. Every so often it seems that major dealers like to clear the decks and mount a selected high-profile sale. LASSCO did so at Dreweatts and among the many unusual items was one particular lot that caught my eye.

The piece in question was a carved oak top-rail from a gate, and, as the brass plaque on the fancy curved and foliate, fruit-carved piece attested, it had come from a rather important pair of gates that were once sited at Sir Christopher Wren's Temple Bar. (The plaque read: 'TOP OF THE GATES OF "TEMPLE BAR" DESIGNED BY WREN AFTER THE FIRE OF LONDON IN 1666. IT WAS TAKEN DOWN BY JOHN MOWLEM & CO UNDER THE SUPERINTENDENCE OF G.B. IN 1877 THE YEAR BEFORE HE WAS SHERIFF OF LONDON 7 MIDDLESEX'.)

Dating from between 1669 and 1672, it was at these gates that the monarch's coronation procession would traditionally halt; the Lord Mayor would hand over the City's Sword of State, affirm London's loyalty and let the monarch pass. Unfortunately, although it was the last of the City gates to survive into the 19th century, it was eventually decided to take it down as a result of the vagaries of fashion, allowing for architectural updating and widening of the street. So it was that this spectacular stone gate was taken down stone by stone and eventually given to the London brewer (there were no willing buyers) Sir Henry Meux, who erected 'Temple Bar' in front of his newly acquired home, Theobalds Park and Mansion in Hertfordshire. There in turn it became badly neglected and the Temple Bar Trust was formed to save it and bring it back to London. It was re-erected at Paternoster Square in 2001 at the cost of £2.9 million. The top bar from the gate was a little cheaper at £8,000 but a wonderful little chunk of architectural history, just the same.

Temple bar in its original setting

Tibetan Travesty

The Tibet Expedition of 1903–04 was a little-known, ill-conceived colonial war that the British waged upon the people of Tibet. Under the auspices of deterring Russian interest in the East, the temporary invasion was mounted by British Indian forces. The mission, albeit misguided, battled in seriously adverse weather and across treacherous terrain all the way to Lhasa, the capital, via Gyantse. With the troops being armed with the latest rifles and Maxim machine guns, the campaign eventually led to the death of several thousand badly armed and untrained Tibetan peasants who had bolstered a small and poorly organised elite class of fighting monks, mostly armed with antiquated matchlocks. The British force led by Colonel Sir Francis Younghusband largely comprised Gurkha and Pathan troops suited to high-altitude conditions: some 3,000 troops in total with around 7,000 Sherpas.

Apparently, much of the problem had revolved around the fact that the Tibetans and the Dalai Lama would not respond to British requests for talks and the British obviously took being ignored very seriously. The first stand-off led to between 600 and 700 Tibetans being mowed down by the withering fire of Maxim machine guns. This action was apparently prompted by a misunderstanding, or more likely the refusal of the Tibetans to leave their defensive positions in a pass – or their refusal to fight at all, provoking a frustrated desire to attack. It became known as the massacre of Chumik Shenko.

The results of the entire campaign were largely inconclusive. A treaty was duly drawn up after the Tibetans were formally defeated. It was mostly irrelevant or untenable for the Tibetan people and even British public opinion was starting to find such colonial behaviour distasteful. Many condemned the war as, in the words of writer Dinesh Lal, a 'deliberate massacre of unarmed men'.

As an interesting footnote to this ink stain on the blotter of British imperialism, it was a collection of photographs and associated material that came up for auction at the salerooms of Henry Aldridge in Devizes that brought the little-known campaign back to the attention of historians. Captain William Charles Hayman, ADC (Aide de Camp) of the aforementioned Colonel Younghusband, had amassed some 140 photographs, which had come down through the family by direct descent. Most were unpublished and interest was keen as the collection realised a sturdy £10,000. Other artefacts brought back by Captain Hayman included various religious icons. Speculation was rife that the wanton destruction of Tibetan temples and buildings had led to looting during the campaign. Two bronze figures of Mahakala and Ushnishavijaya made £65,000 and £38,000 respectively.

Jolly Roger

It wasn't just pirate vessels that carried the Jolly Roger. In the Second World War submarines carried it too, and one such flag was the centre of keen bidding in a recent sale at Bosleys Auctioneers of Marlow.

Apart from the fact that these flags are ordinarily very collectable, this particular one had come from HMS *Seraph*, a vessel involved in several covert operations, including one of the most bizarre undercover plans of the war. Operation Mincemeat involved placing top-secret but totally false information into the hands of the Spanish authorities, who although ostensibly neutral at the time were more than likely, under Franco, to pass the plans to German intelligence. In order to do this they used the body of a dead man, whom they called 'Major William Martin'. The mission was meticulously planned and Martin was made to appear as if he had died in an air accident with a case containing 'top-secret plans' manacled to his wrist designed to trick the Germans into believing an Allied invasion was set for Greece. The body was deposited from the submarine off the coast of Spain, complete with fake pictures of his girl-friend 'Pam', a girl who really worked for MI5. The body was carried by the tide and discovered by a local Spanish fisherman and, just as planned, was duly handed over to the authorities. The ruse had a significant impact on the success of Allied operations and the Germans diverted troops away from Sicily where the Allies invaded two months later. The corpse of 'Major William Martin' was apparently that of a Welsh tramp by the name of Glyndwr Michael. The whole episode inspired the film *The Man Who Never Was* and was marvellously described in Ben Macintyre's book of 2010, *Operation Mincemeat: The True Spy Story that Changed the Course of World War II*.

Submarine Jolly Rogers display a number of symbols for 'kills' and operations. This flag had numerous such symbols relating to aircraft and surface vessels as well as daggers for cloak-and-dagger operations. In 1944 a new commander had replaced the flag and the vendor's father, then a junior rating on the submarine, had taken it home. It sold for £14,000.

✧✦❀✦✧

Play Misty for Me

If you've ever had the pleasure of visiting the Natural History Museum in London then you'll be very familiar with the displays of dinosaur skeletons and groups of mesmerised school children. What you might not realise is that the museum's famous 'Dippy' the Diplodocus is actually a plaster cast of the fossil skeleton in the Carnegie Museum of Natural History, Pittsburgh, USA, which is composed of more than one Diplodocus! Complete skeletons are naturally extremely rare and so it was with great anticipation that Summers Place Auctions in Billingshurst, West Sussex, were able to offer the complete 150 million-year-old fossilised skeleton of a female Diplodocus called 'Misty'. It is one of only a few known examples and at seventeen metres long is believed to be the first 'large' dinosaur offered in the UK. Found in Wyoming by the children of the celebrated dinosaur hunter Raimund Albersdörfer, 'Misty' was prepared in a laboratory in Holland before being shipped over to the UK for the 'Evolution' sale. She was sold to the Danish Natural History Museum for a hammer price of £400,000.

Grave Decision

While fears about the trafficking and looting of antiquities continue to cause grave concern, the market for such ancient treasure remains stronger than ever. Given the due diligence exercised by auction houses and dealers, it's imperative that the market continues to be scrutinised in all those areas that might promote the desecration of ancient sites and monuments, known or unknown; however, the legitimate trade in well documented and provenanced objects has proved to be a valuable boost to the art world given some recent results. Following the success of the sale of a Late Period Dynasty greywacke (type of stone) statue of Isis in 2012 for a record £3.75 million, Christie's decided to relocate their antiquities sales back to their showcase King Street rooms in South Kensington. This was seen as a boost to and reaffirmation of the market *and* the profile of antiquities sales in London. Antiquities have also seen a boost as an interior design statement, both at the lower end and at the highest sector of the market. Some strong results were recorded recently, including the Christie's sale of a superb Cycladic female marble figure for £180,000. However, this was far from being a record following their sale of a Cycladic figure in New York in 2010 – that example achieved a world record £10 million! Another recent gem was a superb Etruscan alabaster cinerary urn carved in relief and illustrating the chariot race of Pelops and Oinomaos. It realised £75,000. It was not unlike a slightly distressed one I once found in the back garden of a house ...

In 2009 I wrote a pre-sale review for the sale of Yves Saint Laurent's collection. It was a wonderfully eclectic and stylish sale and caused a great stir among collectors with very high prices achieved over the two-day dispersal. One item was a metre-high Roman marble torso of an athlete, which sold at the time for £979,765. However, 'celebrity' sales often attract increased bidding. It was re-offered in a more recent Christie's sale and sold for less at £800,000.

Popular among decorators and collectors are good Attic vases and when attributable to certain painters they tend to fetch premium prices. An example depicting a nude athlete and a draped youth dating from around 500–450BC and ascribed to the Alkimachos painter realised a healthy

£95,000. And if busts are your thing, as they tend to be among connoisseurs and decorators, Bonhams topped one of their recent antiquities sales with a wonderful crisp Roman marble head and shoulders of Gaius Caesar for £310,000.

If all of this seems a little too 'rich' for your pocket there are plenty of more affordable pieces around. Why not a little Greek Xenon-ware pottery guttus (a form of small vessel with a spout used for pouring oils or unguents) dating from the 4th century BC? Yours for a mere £220.

Torc of the Town

A few years ago an amateur treasure hunter found a large coiled object in a bog near Co. Fermanagh in Northern Ireland. Apparently, his initial reaction was that he had found an old car spring but having sat on his find for a couple of years he was surprised to see something similar in a magazine and realised that what he had was rather more important. The object is in fact a 3,000-year-old gold torc, a piece of jewellery formed from twisted gold (*torc* from the Latin 'to twist'). After a treasure inquest was subsequently held, the find has been heralded as 'one of the most spectacular single objects of prehistoric jewellery ever found in

Ireland'. Interestingly, it cannot be worn in its present state because it has been turned into a long spiral rather than its original form as a large single loop. This may be because it was ritually despoiled but the reasons aren't altogether clear. Despite this, it remains a valuable historic treasure and has now gone on display in the 'Early Peoples' gallery of the Ulster Museum.

Origin of Species

Julia Margaret Cameron was a 19th-century female photographer – a rare breed in the Victorian age. Born in Calcutta in 1815, she took up photography rather late in life at the age of 48 after being given a camera as a present. She is notable for her portraits of celebrities and Arthurian styled pictures which capture her subjects in an intimate and hitherto previously uncharted way. Her close-cropped soft-focus and sometimes blurred ethereal images were a meticulous evolution that was sometimes ridiculed by her contemporaries. However, her style was popular among her sitters, despite the fact that she worked outside the conventions of a typical studio and apparently took many plates in what could be a very time-consuming process. Her meticulous nature also meant that she registered all her photographs with the copyright office, a major reason for the survival of so many examples of her work in what was a relatively short career of eleven years.

At her home on the Isle of Wight, she received numerous famous artists, actors, writers, academics and politicians. She was heavily influenced in style by the Pre-Raphaelite movement and it seems that many contemporaries saw her photographic interpretations as mere pastiches, although she viewed them as an art form – which they are. In 1875 she moved back east to Ceylon (Sri Lanka) where photography was more difficult to practise. Scarcity of materials and lack of access to her retinue of subjects meant that she took fewer photographs and very little survives from this period in her life. She died in 1879 of a 'chill'.

Largely forgotten after her death, her work gained in appreciation with the publication of a book by Helmut Gernsheim in 1948. Recognition for her place in photographic history subsequently mounted and she is now both respected and valued as an important influence on the course of modern photography. In some cases, her portraits are the only known photographic representations of various prominent personages of the Victorian period and are hence historically very important.

Dominic Winter Auctioneers were lucky enough to be able to offer a trademark Cameron portrait of Charles

Darwin signed by both Cameron and the great man himself. The photograph had apparently been passed down through the family of Joseph Parslow, butler and manservant to Darwin for over 30 years. Naturally (if you'll excuse the pun), it made a hefty £28,000.

Julia Cameron's portrait of Darwin (unsigned!)

Peking Duck

Still on the subject of photography – we've all heard of famous war photographers such as Tim Page who made his name in the Vietnam War but probably few people have heard of Felice (or Felix) Beato. Born in Venice in 1832 of British parentage, he spent most of his life travelling the world taking photographs and is regarded as one of the first war photographers or 'photojournalists'. Beato is well known for his images of east Asia and particularly China where he took a number of photographs during the second Opium War. Mostly taken in 1860, Beato would sell the photographs to interested parties, including soldiers. Sotheby's were able to offer one such collection purchased at the time by a lieutenant in the Royal Engineers. The eighteen photographs formed a perfect visual narrative of the campaign in which the lieutenant had taken part, including views of the Summer Palace before and after its destruction and a superb six-plate panorama of the Forbidden City. It was during this campaign that so many imperial treasures were looted by the French and British, some of which have subsequently been finding their way back on to the market with heavy price tags in recent years. The aforementioned set of photographs proved to be of great monetary value too, realising £180,000.

Yankee Doodle

At roughly the same time that the British and French were giving the Chinese a major lesson in imperialist attitudes to resistant foreigners, the Americans were in the throes of their catastrophic civil war. Just as the invention of photography had led to the visual record taken by Beato, several photographers were recording the events of the war in America. Many of these were compiled at the end of the conflict in 1866 in two volumes by Alexander Gardner called *Photographic Sketchbook of the War*. The *Sketchbook* comprises 100 albumen prints, some of a rather macabre nature including a famous photograph by John Reekie showing a

An image from *Photographic Sketchbook of the War*

burial party of black men collecting a grisly cargo of semi-clothed skeletons from the battlefield of Gaines' Mill and Cold Harbor in Virginia. The dead had lain fallen for over ten months before burial because at nigh-on 60,000 casualties, the locals were unable to cope with the sheer scale of the task. The collection of photographs, originally produced commercially, did not sell well at the time, but a recent example sold for £99,250.

A Big Fiddle

Henry Aldridge of Devizes are renowned for their specialist auctions of maritime-related memorabilia, particularly from the *Titanic*. Collectors of *Titanic* material are well known for their determination and despite the momentous objects sold by Henry Aldridge in recent years it seemed like nothing was likely to top their record-breaking sale of the large hand-drawn plan of the ship that was used at the official enquiry. It sold for £220,000 in 2011.

The survival of the violin played by bandmaster Wallace Hartley as the ship went down in 1912 seemed like a leap too far for many sceptical onlookers. The violin, said to have been strapped to the body of Hartley, was recovered in a leather bag (which is still with it). It took over seven years to verify the authenticity of the instrument using various tests and provenance material.

The story of Hartley has become folkloric, one of the most iconic tales of heroism from the doomed ship as he, along with the band, is said to have played 'Nearer My God to Thee' as the stricken vessel went down. I live just a few miles away from the Devizes saleroom and after a quick phone call, was lucky enough to be able to arrange a visit and hold the violin. Few items could have been charged with such an emotive feel and my thirteen-year-old daughter found her teacher's face rather incredulous when she recounted how she had handled the violin from the *Titanic* in her school holidays. (I suppose that's one benefit of having a father who works on the *Antiques Roadshow*!)

Although estimated at £200,000–300,000, bidding opened at £50 so that a friend of the auctioneers would have the chance to bid – a nice personal touch. However, the increments soon increased and the bidding spiralled upwards, settling at £900,000 (plus 15 per cent commission). This is a record for any item associated with the ship and I'm not sure that there's any other object that will ever come close.

Headline News

We like to bemoan the state of the media and the tabloid press but when did it all begin? Firstly, it's necessary to define what a newspaper is, and there are many criteria for doing so. Most agree that the main factors include news content and publicity based upon an ability to regularly report and update news, allied to a regular frequency of publication. The World Association of Newspapers apparently accepts that applying such criteria makes *Relation aller Fürnemmen und gedenckwürdigen Historien* ('Account of all distinguished and commemorable news'), published in Strasbourg by Johann Carolus in 1609, the first true newspaper. However, there are those who would disagree on the basis of format, as *Relation* still looks rather like a book.

The oldest still-published newspaper in the world is the *Ordinari Post Tijdender*, a Swedish 'rag' that has forsaken its original format of 1645 and is now published online. The first English newspaper is held to be the *Oxford Gazette*: number 1 was published on 7 November, 1665. It was so named due to its place of printing: the *Gazette* was published in Oxford as a result of London being in the grip of the plague. Charles II had moved his court to Oxford to avoid infection. Due to the fact that very few people could read, it's thought that the newspaper was posted to around a hundred recipients, hence its rarity. The plague is casually dealt with among the other political, religious and military news, with a matter-of-fact reference to 1,050 people having died that week!

Mullock's Auctioneers of Ludlow were able to offer a copy at one of their specialist manuscript sales, along with several later copies of the *Gazette* – which, still published, became the *London Gazette* when relocated to the capital after the plague – but at an estimate of £12,000–15,000, the media hype was not quite sufficient for it to find a buyer. However, that's one newspaper that won't find its way into the recycling.

Scrap Metal

philistine

noun

1. a person who is hostile or indifferent to culture or the arts

—Oxford Dictionary

Arguments will always rage about what constitutes art or whether some art is good at all. We all have our own opinions and tolerance of the opinions of others is important.

Some intolerance comes from a lack of understanding of processes; some from a general lack of interest; some from a social misunderstanding of different aspects of art. In short, education can make a world of difference in being able to make a reasoned judgement. Frankly, I know what I like and my likes are remarkably eclectic, but despite that I have on several occasions maligned certain artistic works (mainly 20th century). Mind you, I hope that I have done so with a fairly comprehensive understanding of the route that artists take in order to arrive at certain decisions, rather than deriding works simply because I don't like them. Safe to say, I am not a philistine and if I were I would definitely be in the wrong profession!

Throughout history, people have destroyed art. The term 'philistine', with its biblical roots, seems to have come into common usage in the 17th century, and by the early 19th century generally described people who were termed 'indifferent to culture', but not necessarily malicious. Reasons for destroying art have been varied: invasion, political dissension, iconoclasm, idealism and downright vengefulness, to name just a few. Such intolerance is still rife in certain parts of the world. Sadly, here too, over the last few years the art world has seen an increasingly destructive pattern emerge, perhaps perpetrated by people we would like to call philistines. Realistically, the pattern of destruction and vandalism wreaked on several high-profile artworks has more to do with the price of scrap metal than the aesthetic knowledge of the criminals who carry out such wanton destruction. As the world's super-heated economies thirst for the raw materials that fuel their industrial engines, the value of many such commodities has risen dramatically. Copper, lead and bronze have become targets for the senseless destruction of everything from war memorials to manhole covers, a problem that is estimated to be costing the economy more than £700 million a year.

Bronze, being the preferred metal for casting sculpture, has been a particularly popular target for thieves and some of the pieces now lost are irreplaceable. In 2005, Henry Moore's two tonne 'Reclining Figure' was stolen from the Moore Foundation in Hertfordshire. Valued at £3 million, it was never recovered but subsequent police investigations drew the conclusion that it had been cut up on the night it was taken and sold to a scrapyard for as little as £1,500. It was then shipped out of the country and probably ended up in China.

Although some major works are definitely stolen to order, many are sadly being broken up for a fraction of their actual monetary worth. What's more, numerous works are taken from public places where their communal enjoyment is robbed from the wider community. In 2012, two young men aged nineteen and 22 stole 'Working Model for Sundial', again from the Henry Moore Foundation (their security has since been beefed up). They returned four days later and ripped another bronze from its plinth, 'Upright Motive No. 7', and took the base. 'Sundial', valued at £500,000, was sold for £48 scrap and the base was sold for £182.60 scrap. The pieces were recovered but cost £13,000 to repair. The pair were jailed for a year but had absolutely no idea of the significance of what they had perpetrated.

The most recent thefts include another Moore, 'Standing Figure', from the Glenkiln Park sculpture park near Dumfries, set up by Sir William Keswick between 1951 and 1976. The bronze, dating from 1950, was in a remote location and although of considerable value was on public display.

Much more audacious was the theft from Dulwich Park in south London of 'Two Forms (Divided Circle)' by iconic British sculptress Barbara Hepworth, another large bronze sculpture which had been in the park for 40 years. Although insured for £500,000 it was one of only six cast and was undoubtedly worth more. Scrap value: £750.

These are just a few of the artworks that have suffered at the hands of the metal thieves. Few of us get to hear of the much larger amount of material that is ripped from memorials, churches and town squares despite the best efforts of those who are trying to stop them. New draft guidelines are afoot to hand down tougher sentences to thieves who target cultural property and it is intended that the legislation will factor in 'the broader impact of the theft on the victim, such as emotional distress.' Let's hope this comes to fruition.

<figure>⚜</figure>

The Man From Xian

I love a surreal experience and a recent knock on the front door proved to be just that as I found myself smiling at a Chinese couple who spoke absolutely no English. Luckily they had an iPhone, which makes a fairly reasonable translator in such situations. It turned out that they had done an internet search and arrived in the hope of adding to a burgeoning collection of optical instruments over in China. I explained that I had been to Xian and as it happened that was their home town. Although slightly hampered by the pace of the iPhone translator, we had a very convivial time and I was humorously coerced into selling a couple of pairs of binoculars from the six pairs housed in a nearby drawer (I rarely have just one of anything). Value wasn't the real issue and I was pleased to send the couple on their way content that they had added to the collection over in Xian. Nice people.

Whether or not they would have been interested in an

early Italian binocular telescope sold in a Christie's 'Science, Travel and Natural History' sale would have very much depended on their budget. The inscription *Petrus Patronus Sac:caes et cat. Maies. Opticus, Medlani, 1719* marked it out as an optical instrument by the Milanese maker Pietro Patroni. These are exceedingly rare. This example was once supposedly owned by the Conte Donato Silva di Biandrate – a patron of Patroni and a scholar. The tripod stand variously decorated with Chinoiserie scenes completed the ensemble. A catalogue inclusion reminding potential buyers that the importation of certain materials from endangered species, including ivory, should be taken into account, due to the fact that the telescope has ivory lens mounts (a factor now heavily relevant in determining the sale of many antique items, especially to America) didn't deter interested parties from taking it to £338,500, including commission.

Banknote

A few years ago we filmed an *Antiques Roadshow* on Guernsey in the Channel Islands. One of the items I enthused about was a rare £1 note worth around £3,000, made even more enthralling by the fact that the owner's father had once had a whole carrier bag full of them – alas, given away as souvenirs long before they became valuable.

Collecting banknotes is a popular pastime and can cost dearly, so forget the face value and consider some of these recent results. Sold by Spink's at their 'World Banknotes Auction', a very rare Bermuda Government £5 from 1 August 1941 with the serial number A000001 realised an inflationary £38,000. A 1901 Falkland Islands five shilling note, number 00001, made £26,000. Another interesting example was a Government of Iraq 50 fils note which featured King Faisal as a child. It was perforated with the word

The Grand Watermelon

'SPECIMEN' and made £38,000. These were just a few of the high prices achieved. However, these pale entirely into insignificance when we take into account a note sold at auction in Chicago by the Central States Numismatic Society (CSNS). Known as the 'Grand Watermelon', the $1,000 bill, dating from 1891, is one of only two known to exist. The other is in the Smithsonian. It features a portrait of the US General George Meade and when last sold in 1944 it had made $1,350. This time it realised a hyper-inflationary $2.5 million.

Portal in a Storm

I find it quite hard to keep up with the continual innovations of the internet. The mass of information seems to sometimes swamp and continually divert, sending you off in distracted directions, further down endless paths of discovery and sometimes obscurity. It's a wonderful tool but an all-consuming nightmare for the curious – like me.

Needless to say, I was unable to resist a look at the new Amazon Art site, which although currently aimed mainly at the American market provides yet another portal for potential buyers. True, the site is eminently searchable by several criteria including subject, style and price. Tickets range from \$30 to several million, although the price-search window didn't cope well with figures at that sort of level. Also, and I'm sure this might be the case for most serious buyers, I do prefer to see my purchases in the flesh. Call me old-fashioned in that respect but this new venture seems like a rather cynical ploy to grab a part of an already well catered-for market and it'll be interesting to see if it expands into the UK.

Blue John

Derbyshire Blue John is a semi-precious mineral with a heavy crystalline structure characteristically coloured in purple-blue and yellow bands. It's a distinctive fluorite only found in the Treak Cliff and Blue John Caverns at Castleton in Derbyshire. Although different forms of it occur in other parts of the world, the colouration of the Derbyshire fluorite has made it much prized as an ornamental stone, perhaps since Roman times, although its documented use dates mainly from the mid-18th century when it came into favour as the basis for decorative fireplace panels. Early known examples include panels used by Robert Adam, the famous Neoclassical architect, at Kedleston Hall near Derby.

Because of the structure of the stone, it has to undergo a process of drying for at least a year. After heating it was then put into pine resin (now epoxy resin) which would replace the air gaps in the stone and give stability for cutting and turning. Subsequent 're-dips' could be carried out if necessary. Vases, candelabra and urns were popular forms in the 18th and early 19th centuries and are much sought by collectors. Many were mounted with ormolu and such examples can command high prices at auction. A pair of beautifully mounted vases were sold by Tennants Auctioneers of Leyburn in 2012 for £120,000.

Current output from the historic mines is probably only around half a tonne a year and is limited to local production. Given the finite supplies, it was with some relief that a rumoured lost seam, mentioned 70 years earlier by a former miner, was recently rediscovered, ensuring the continuation of a truly Derbyshire-based craft.

Life Drawing

Good artists copy, great artists steal
—PABLO PICASSO

Early mechanical toys are very collectable and I've had the pleasure over many years in the antiques business of winding up some wonderful examples. They've ranged from the animated pouncing tigers, walking elephants, rabbits in cabbages and complicated tableaux made by 19th-century firms such as Roullet et Decamps to the cheap tinplate clockwork creations of myriad European and, later, Japanese companies.

Favourites include one particular variety and although I often deter my daughter from spending too much time on YouTube, it can be useful – you might find it interesting to enter the words 'Philip Vielmetter Clown Artist' and watch the video that comes up. It shows a wonderfully ingenious lithographed tin toy called 'The Artist'. Made by the company of Philip Vielmetter Mechanische Werkstatten of Berlin, it dates from around 1895. The brightly coloured tinplate clown (packed in a wooden crate) sits in front of an easel. Double-sided cams fit into the base and, with a small piece of paper attached to his easel, the clown draws a number of different portraits using a piece of graphite. Depending on the cam, Queen Victoria, Napoleon and

Balzac are part of his repertoire. These he executes with amazing finesse and you can imagine the entertainment he provided. Frankly, he would have been expensive and perhaps 'toy' is too demeaning a term for an object that would have more likely been the plaything of a wealthier person.

Another, similar version of the toy was made by the English company of Joseph Walker of Birmingham. A more conventional-looking artist type, 'he' has a less colourful appearance with a gold lacquer-style finish, but also executes a number of reasonable portraits including one of Lord Wellington – which can also be seen on YouTube by typing in 'Joseph Walker Mechanical Drawing Artist'. Antiquity and modern media meeting to provide an entertaining moment! The most recent example of the clown artist was sold at Bonhams for £2,200.

Signed and Sealed

Never in a million years would I profess to be an expert on Chinese reign marks. It's a complicated field with many subtle differences between calligraphic and seal marks used over thousands of years in many different and often reverential ways, which means that the reign mark often doesn't match the age of the piece. That's why items in auction catalogues are often described as being 'of period and mark', indicating that the mark is correct. Given the continually unpredictable nature of the market and the uncertainty in dating many Chinese ceramics, buyers are often left to make up their own minds and it's then that we often see sky-high prices occurring.

Obviously, it's quite useful if you have a mark on an object and the Chinese practice of painting reign marks on porcelain is very helpful. This was particularly popular in the Ming (1368–1644) and Qing (1644–1911) dynasties. However, as you can see, both were quite long periods and the difference between a vase that was made in 1650 or 1911 can be considerable. Below, as a beginner's insight into what the subject entails, is a list of the main dynasties, followed by reproductions of the various marks that can be found on porcelain from the Ming and Qing periods.

Xia (2205–1575BC): The first dynasty in China.

Shang (1570–1045BC): The Shang ruled much of the area along the Yellow River. Their last capital city was the great city of Yin.

Zhou (1045–256BC): The longest-ruling dynasty in the history of China, the Zhou first used the Mandate of Heaven to justify their rule. Much of the land was ruled by feudal lords who were relatives of the Zhou family.

Qin (221–206BC): The beginning of the Chinese Empire; Qin Shi Huang became the first Chinese Emperor. Although this was a short dynasty much was accomplished, including the beginning of the Great Wall; standards were set for weights, measures, and money.

Han (206BC–AD220): The Han dynasty established the civil service to create a strong and organised government. Paper and porcelain were invented during this time. The Han also embraced Confucianism, poetry and literature.

Six Dynasties (AD222–581): A period of time where China was not united under a single leader.

Sui (AD589–618): The Sui united China again under one rule. They also expanded the Great Wall and built the Grand Canal.

Tang (AD618–907): A period of peace and prosperity, the Tang rule is sometimes known as the Golden Age of Ancient China. Arts, literature, and technology all flourished. The capital city Chang'an became the world's largest city.

Five Dynasties (AD907–960): A peasant rebellion took down the Tang dynasty and ushered in a period of division.

Song (AD960–1279): Reunited under the Song, China became a world leader in science and technology, including inventions such as gunpowder and the compass.

Yuan (AD1279–1368): After the Mongols defeated the Song in a long war, Kublai Khan, a Mongol leader, established the Yuan dynasty.

Ming (AD1368–1644): The last of the *great* Chinese dynasties, the Ming finished the Great Wall and built the Forbidden City, an enormous palace for the Emperor. The Ming came to power by overthrowing the rule of the Mongols.

Qing (AD1644–1911): The final imperial dynasty of China, one that lasted almost 300 years but inevitably crumbled in the wake of major cultural upheaval and aggressive foreign intervention. This led to the abdication of the last emperor on 12 February 1912.

YONGLE
1403–1424

年 永
製 樂

XUANDE
1426–1435

德　大
年　明
製　宣

CHENGHUA
1465–1487

化　大
年　明
製　成

HONGZHI
1488–1505

治　大
年　明
製　弘

ZHENGDE
1506–1521

德　大
年　明
製　正

JIAJING
1522–1566

靖　大
年　明
製　嘉

LONGQING
1567–1572

慶　大
年　明
製　隆

WANLI
1573–1619

曆　大
年　明
製　萬

TIANQI
1621–1627

啟　大
年　明
製　夫

Ming dynasty reign marks

SHUNZHI
1644–1661

天清順
清順
年
製

順治
治年
製

KANGXI
1662–1722

熙大清康
年
製

康熙

YONGZHENG
1723–1735

正大清雍
年
製

雍正

QIANLONG
1736–1795

隆大清乾
年
製

乾隆

JIAQING
1796–1820

年嘉慶
製

嘉慶

DAOGUANG
1821–1850

光大清道
年
製

道光

XIANFENG
1851–1861

豐大清咸
年
製

咸豐

TONGZHI
1862–1873

治大清同
年
製

同治

GHANGXU
1874–1908

緒大清光
年
製

光緒

HONGXIAN
1909–1912

統大清宣
年
製

宣統

Qing dynasty reign marks

Trench Warfare

As a child I was a typical boy. I enjoyed spending hours building fortresses out of my Pennybrix (an old type of construction set), setting up rows of plastic soldiers then launching assaults with all sorts of homemade siege engines, elastic band-powered catapults and die-cast field guns – the latter mostly made by Britains.

The name is synonymous with toy soldiers and the company was founded by William Britain Jr in 1893. He developed a process of hollow-casting lead figures, revolutionising the production of toy soldiers, which until then had mainly been made as 'flats' (two-dimensional flat figures) or heavy, solid three-dimensional figures. William Britain & Sons became the industry leaders and by the 1930s were producing around 20 million figures and die-cast toys a years. Their extensive military range, which included boxed sets, vehicles, field guns and diorama accessories, was complemented by farmyards, circuses, zoos and film- and comic book-related items.

Although I was good at constructing my own miniature military installations, I did yearn for some of the purpose-made pieces that I jealously eyed up in the local toy shop, and I would not have been the only small boy who noticed Britains' 'New Patent Exploding Trench', launched at the famous Hamley's toy shop in 1915. The model trench was made of wood and stiffened painted fabric and had a patent mechanism (no. 3189) which had an explosive effect. By way of explanation, here are the manufacturer's own operation instructions:

> Place the flattened end of the flagstaff in the socket made for it, then raise the hammer until it catches the base of the flag socket and remains upright; place a cap in the capholder and mount the soldiers along the trench.
>
> The flag should then be fired at by one of Britain's 4.7 Naval Guns, when, on securing a hit the trench will immediately explode with a loud report.

Just in case you were wondering, the 4.7 Naval Gun was the Britains toy version of a 4.7 inch naval gun converted to field artillery use on distinctive metal plate wheels.

Unfortunately, the timing of the launch of the Exploding Trench could not have been more ill-conceived. With the First World War beginning to send home increasing reports of the terrible casualties in this new form of 'machine age' trench warfare, the initial optimism of the pre-war rhetoric had quickly been superseded by a new reality and the idea of countless soldiers actually dying in the trenches forced a public outcry over the sale of the toy. Its withdrawal meant that relatively few were sold and it is now regarded as one of the Holy (not holey) Grails of the lead soldier collecting market. Less than a handful have come up for sale in the last 30 years but one that unusually made its way over to the USA was recently offered at Old Toy Soldier Auctions in Pittsburgh. It realised an explosive $6,000 – that's around £4,000.

Goldfinger

I was born in 1964. It was a good year for classic films: *My Fair lady*, *A Fist Full of Dollars*, *Zulu*, *Mothra vs. Godzilla*, *Dr. Strangelove*, *The Pink Panther* and, of course, *Goldfinger* (I use the word 'good' from a purely personal perspective). James Bond was filling the cinemas and his gadget-ridden Aston Martin DB5 thrilled audiences, particularly children.

Corgi, the Swansea-based die-cast toy vehicle manufacturer also landed an extraordinary coup that year. Their chief rival, Dinky, had been slower at picking up on the idea of licensing. Corgi had grabbed the concept of tying in the sale of their die-cast vehicles with films, comics and television with vigour. Their head designer was Marcel van Cleemput (who died in March 2013) and it was he who was responsible for Corgi's large and varied output. Other companies were generally taking about two years to put their concepts into the shops but due to van Cleemput's energy Corgi were turning around designs from drawing board to production line within a year. Van Cleemput also realised that gimmicks sold toy cars and this was reflected in the ingenuity of many of Corgi's vehicles.

So what was their coup of 1964? James Bond's DB5! For a small die-cast vehicle, it was packed with gimmicks and as a boy I was enthralled by the ejector seat, pop-up bulletproof screen and expanding wheel hubs. Unfortunately, I was only four days old when the film got its British release so I ended up with a 'second issue' DB5; however, I later acquired a gold first issue.

The car was a smash hit. It was the biggest selling toy of 1964 and went on to sell over 3 million units. Call it nostalgia, but irrespective of the high production levels, the car is very collectable and many people (mainly men) view these childhood toys with some affection. Consequently they are prepared to pay large amounts of money to grab back a slice of that rose-tinted past.

Mint is what makes big money and it's rarely that trade or merchant packs come on to the market. For obvious reasons, old shop stock is scarce but C&T Auctioneers in Rochester offered such a pack featuring six shrink-wrapped DB5s complete with a note under the polythene to the shopkeeper stating, in English, French, German,

Italian and Swedish:

C.261 – James Bond Car

Mr. Retailer,

A REMINDER!

The 'Secret Instructions' are packed in the compartment in the base of every inner display stand.

Please make sure that every young purchaser realizes this.

The pack had been purchased by the vendor some eighteen years ago at a time when several appeared as the former property of an old Corgi sales rep. It would be interesting to know what they cost back then; alas, I don't have that information, but interest was high and they sold for a rewarding £5,500.

The Knowledge

The Chancery Lane Safe Deposit Company opened in 1876. It was a state-of-the-art secure storage facility comprised of rooms with steel-reinforced 1.2 metre-thick walls, three storeys underground. The building received a direct hit during the Second World War and was almost completely destroyed but the vaults were unscathed. In 1953, they became the London Silver Vaults, housing a number of businesses that have continued to remain in the hands of several generations of silver dealers. The whereabouts of the vaults are a prerequisite part of a London cab driver's 'Knowledge'. Having celebrated their 50th anniversary in 2013, the vaults are renowned as 'the largest single collection of silver for sale in the world'.

In a Jam

The golliwog is a black character that originated in children's books of the late 19th century. It's a subject that stirs all sorts of passions for all sorts of reasons, not least that it is regarded by many as a racist representation of black Africans. Other people see it as a culturally nostalgic reminder of their childhoods, a harmless rag doll that was both a positive and a comforting character. The racial connotations of gollies, as they now tend to be known, have led to a number of high-profile incidents over the years, including a lady who alleged that she was arrested by police in Stockport for displaying one in her window and Mrs Thatcher's daughter Carol being sacked from the BBC's *The One Show* for making a remark about the tennis player, Jo-Wilfried Tsonga looking like one. In her defence she maintained that she was referring to the golly motifs that she remembered from her childhood on jars of Robertson's jam. This is perhaps where the nub of the problem lies, for society had been conditioned by such images throughout people's childhoods and especially by their use as an advertising tool and a branding icon. To be honest, in all innocence, many people probably never drew a parallel between gollies and people, either rightly or wrongly, but what is certain is that people were eventually forced to think about it.

Robertson's was founded in the 19th century by James Robertson of Paisley. He alighted on a way of using bitter Seville oranges to make marmalade, the brand that we all know as Golden Shred. The idea of using gollies as an advertising gimmick started in 1910 and by the 1920s the use of enamelled golly brooches had been suggested by H. Miller, a skilled enameller from Birmingham's Jewellery Quarter. The first design appeared in 1928 as the 'Golfer'. The rest is history.

By the 1980s the badges were being made of acrylic and they were finally phased out in 2001. The brand also spawned many other related objects, including plaster golly musician figures, but popularity had waned among the younger fraternity and towards the end the gimmick was perhaps mainly propped up by the older generation who regarded gollies with nostalgia rather than as potentially controversial. It's thought that over 20 million were dispatched to collectors.

A definitive collection owned by a gentleman called Mike Martin was recently dispersed by Vectis Auctions.

Mid-20th-century advertisement for Robertson's
Golden Shred marmalade, featuring the iconic golly

Although most are worth just a few pounds, highlights from the sale included a pre-war 'Northants Cricketer' golly which made £700, a pre-war 'Footballer' golly which made £320 and a 1937 George VI Coronation golly which made £540.

Deathly Pallor

It may sound macabre but I have a strong interest in death masks. Among the few I own are a plaster cast of Napoleon – not particularly attractive in death – and a far more regal-looking pottery version of Beethoven, resplendent with a gilded laurel on his head. It was with interest that I noticed that a death mask of the composer Gustav Mahler was scheduled to be sold at a sale of manuscripts to include music at Sotheby's in London. The mask was one of possibly four or five examples taken from a cast made by Mahler's father-in-law Carl Moll, who was present at his bedside when he passed away. It sold for £30,000.

Boom or Bust

Adam Smith (1723–1790) is known as the 'father of modern economics'. Born in Kirkcaldy, Scotland, he was a philosopher and a pioneer of economic theory. He is credited with the rationale behind the idea of the free market economy and the theory that competition could lead to economic prosperity. As a leading luminary in the Scottish enlightenment he promoted the principles of free speech, liberty and reason. Apart from countless essays and papers, which he mostly had destroyed just before he died, he wrote two great works: *The Theory of Moral Sentiments* (1759) and *An Enquiry into the Nature and Causes of the Wealth of Nations* (1776), usually known as *The Wealth of Nations*. Apparently, Mrs Thatcher is said to have carried a copy of the latter in her handbag, although I cannot confirm the truth or otherwise of this! *Wealth of Nations* is also cited as one of the top 100 most important Scottish books of all time.

Smith was a clever man, a polymath in reality and several of his works were published posthumously. Copies of his work are very sought after. *Wealth of Nations* is highly prized and several copies of the two volumes have come to market in the last couple of years. Values have wavered at between £43,640 and £55,000 for second and third editions but a copy of the first edition recently sold for £92,190. However, the record still remains at £157,250 (including commission) realised by Christie's in 2010 for the 'Foljambe' copy owned by the MP Francis Ferrand Foljambe (1749–1814). Interesting to think what Smith would have made of the value of his book and the free market economy!

Clock Watcher

Breguet: it's a name synonymous with quality and luxury, a watch brand founded in Paris in 1775 by Abraham-Louis-Breguet. The marque is now owned by The Swatch Group but is one of the oldest surviving watchmakers in the world and can lay claim to a number of groundbreaking inventions, including the famous tourbillon mechanism which helps to diminish the effects of gravity by mounting the escapement and balance wheel in a rotating cage. Rather like a gyroscope in principle, this helps to improve accuracy.

The history of Breguet's company and his client list reads like a who's who through history, including most European monarchs since the late 18th century, Napoleon, Churchill, etc. Possibly his most magnificent and complicated early creation was a watch commissioned for Marie Antoinette. The 'Breguet no. 160 Grand Complication' incorporated just about every known function possible in that period of watchmaking and included a clock, perpetual calendar, minute repeater, thermometer, chronograph, parechute (anti-shock device) and a chime. It's a masterpiece encased in a rock crystal and gold case. Work commenced on the watch in 1782 and it was finished in 1827 by his son, four years after Breguet's death. Of course, Marie Antoinette never saw the watch finished – she was executed 34 years prior!

Until 1983, the watch formed part of the collection of the L.A. Mayer Institute for Islamic Art in Jerusalem. It had originally been part of the David Lionel Salomons collection and was donated along with many other valuable pieces. However, 106 timepieces were stolen that year and it wasn't until 2007 that some were recovered, including the Antoinette watch. The deal for their return was brokered by a lawyer who, for a mere $40,000, arranged for the return of the pieces from an anonymous American woman. She turned out to be the widow of a notorious Israeli thief called Na'aman Diller who had single-handedly raided the museum, which, it turned out, had no functioning alarm. The watch is thought to be worth around $30 million.

From a personal point of view, I was lucky enough, a few years ago to come across an elegant and understated pocket watch in its case – made for the Duke of Wellington's niece. A snip at a mere £10,000.

However, recent records tumbled as an elaborate quarter repeating clock made for the Duc d'Orléans and delivered in 1836, surmounted with a quarter striking gold watch, wooed potential bidders with its highly complicated 'Sympathique' movement and an ability to wind and set the time of the pocket watch at the same time as the clock – incredible! The price was incredible too, at $6 million!

Battle Lines

The Battle of Vigo was a major naval engagement that took place on 23 October 1703. Following a disastrous attempt by an Anglo-Dutch force to capture Cadiz under Admiral George Rooke, the ships were forced to turn back towards England. However, they received intelligence of a heavily laden Spanish treasure fleet returning from the Americas under French escort. It was moored in Vigo Bay in Galicia.

The bay was heavily defended by a French and Spanish contingent with forts, several batteries of guns, and a boom. M. Château-Renault, who had masterminded the defence of the harbour, had also stationed the firepower of seven men-o'-war within the boom and at each end. Due to the width of the entrance, the English and the Dutch were unable to mount a typical naval assault. Instead, 2,000 troops were landed (to deal with the forts and gun batteries) and the boom was rammed, enabling the Allied ships to break through. Many of the French and Spanish set fire to their own ships and a total of six ships were captured by the English and Dutch with nine others either destroyed by fire or run ashore.

Unfortunately for the Allies, most of the silver and gold had already been unloaded and the captured prizes largely consisted of spice, snuff, dyes and hides. However, some of the gold and silver that was recovered, having been delivered to London and recorded by the then Master of the Mint, Sir Isaac Newton, was struck into coins. One particular such coin is called the 'Queen Anne Vigo' and is clearly struck with 'Vigo' under her profile. An example of this rare gold five guinea piece was brought into Gorringes Auctioneers of Lewes. Being in exceptionally fine condition, it set a record for such a coin on what many thought was a 'punchy' estimate of £80,000–12,000. A hammer price of £240,000 soon found sceptics wrong!

Old Cow

The 1924 British Empire Exhibition in Wembley was a huge colonial exposition comprising 58 countries. It was opened on 23 April (St George's Day) by King George V at the cost of £12 million. It was the largest exhibition ever staged anywhere in the world. Naturally, there were representatives from every sector of industry, manufacturing and agriculture and, as is usual, a myriad of promotional giveaways and commemorative items were produced to mark the exhibition. Nestlé were one of the exhibitors.

Nestlé, now the biggest grossing food company in the world, was founded in the 1860s in Switzerland. Incidentally, their first British operation, making milk-based products such as baby food and condensed milk, began in the town of Chippenham where I live, and the original factory – now offices – is one of the few 19th-century riverside premises to survive in the town centre. It is also further remembered for the role of a young woman, Florence Hancock (later Dame Florence Hancock) who at the age of 20 organised a strike which hoped to force a living wage from the owners. It was a bitterly contested protest, the first strike of its type in the town and a majorly symbolic event for the cause of women's rights in the workplace. Known as 'the little milkmaid from Chippenham', Dame Florence Hancock became a major force in the union movement, spending her life working with the Transport & General Workers' Union and becoming the president of the TUC in 1949.

However, I digress! As a promotional item for the exhibition, Nestlé commissioned a series of hollow-cast cows from the famous makers of soldiers and hollow-cast figures, Britains. Known as the 'Map of the World Cow' or 'World Cow', the lead cows were cast with the words 'Nestlés Milk' and 'The World Cow' on their flanks, their bodies cleverly painted with a stylised map of the world. Black and white variants are the most common and realise around £100–150 in good condition. The cow was also issued in a set called the 'Nestlé Home Farm'. These are very rare and the last one that came up for sale, in 2011, made £3,500.

Due to the fact that the figures were mainly painted by

outside pieceworkers, different colourways caused by different interpretations of the specified models sometimes appear. Several such examples, purchased at the 1924 exhibition for three sisters, were subsequently placed in the family's china cabinet; one, in dark brown and white with 'reversed' colours, was exceptionally rare. When this group were recently offered for sale they far exceeded expectations, realising between £950 and £2,000 each. So, next time you are sifting through a pile of old farmyard animals, look out for The World Cow!

Sword Play

My room is like an antique shop, full of junk
and weird stuff. There's a big sword in there.
—FLORENCE WELCH (SINGER AND MUSICIAN)

I have a few swords dotted around the house – as you do. My favourite is a Luristan (Western Iran) bronze sword dating from around 1500BC but I also like a 19th-century cavalry officer's sword that was part of the famous Ken Paul prop hire collection and used in the 1968 film *Charge of the Light Brigade.*

Arms and armour are a buoyant part of the art and antiques market. The craftsmanship and history of many such items often transcends their original purpose so whatever your feelings about the art of war, this really can be about the 'art' of war! However, it's also important to note that arms fall into several different categories which include sporting weapons (hunting and target shooting) and ceremonial material, which includes all manner of highly crafted and beautifully decorated weapons, armour and uniforms that were never meant for anything other than pomp and ceremony.

The sale of art and antiques can be very seasonal and it's often in the interest of many major auction houses and galleries to stage a series of complementary events, sales, lectures and exhibitions. Asian Art in London is a bi-annual event that does just that, bringing together as many as 60 dealers, top auction houses and museums to produce a major splash. It's a formula that works well, attracting connoisseurs from around the world – arms and armour are no exception.

Highlights of the past year include the amazingly rare 14th-century sword from the Mamluk Arsenal at Alexandria, sold by Bonhams. Catalogued as 'probably Italian', the much published sword is one of only four known examples inscribed with the name Amir Faris, an inspector in 840AH (meaning 'after Hijrah' in the Islamic calendar;

this date corresponds to AD1436–7 in the Christian calendar). It came from the collection of E.A. Christensen. It's thought that it was part of an ambassadorial gift from Peter I, ruler of Cyprus and Jerusalem, to the Mamluk rulers of Alexandria. Competition was fierce and the hammer finally came down at £135,000.

Another gem from the collection was an exceptional rare 9th-century Viking sword which had been found in the river Thiele in Switzerland in 1887. It was in excavated condition but provenance and scarcity pushed it to £27,500.

Never far from the action is the 'leading specialist auctioneer' Thomas Del Mar, whose sales have a reputation for bringing some wonderful rarities to market including a £34,000 two-shot belt pistol of 1609 by Valentin Klett of Suhl in Thuringia, a town where firearms are still manufactured to this day. This pistol was a 'wheel-lock' model, so called because of the wheel-shaped mechanism that produces a spark by friction. In fact, this was the first type of self-igniting firearm and a major technological step forward from the burning fuse of the matchlock. This example fired two consecutive charges from the same barrel. Very clever and hence the price!

I was rather taken by the idea of a pair of French 18th-century saluting cannon, which being on their own carriages and quite compact would have made a good pair of decorative additions to a large country house drawing room.

Not quite sure about the saluting, although I'm sure they probably still function! Well priced, I thought at £13,200. Bonhams raised more for a pair of bronze cannon bearing the coat of arms for the Counts of Gavre; the family had raised troops to fight for the Holy Roman Empire and these cannon were catalogued as 'probably 17th century or later'. The carriages were later but together they managed a fairly explosive £18,000. Interestingly, the cannon had previously sold at the famous Hever Castle sale in 1983 for £24,000, which emphasises the higher prices often paid at such high-profile events and dispersals.

Armour is always in demand but offerings can be patchy, mainly due to the rarity of early pieces. Two stunningly decorative suits were sold by Christie's, both 16th-century in style. One, known as a 'black and white' armour due to the tonal finish, sold for £44,000 while the other, a gothic Maximilian-style suit, sold for £20,000 – but note the terminology here as 'style' means that they were not period; both were in fact made as decorative suits to satisfy the tastes of late 19th or early 20th-century collectors. They were perhaps made by the Munich maker Ernst Schmidt and were very good quality.

Period pieces included some rare survivors from those romantic days of jousting, although the state of the armour completely dispels that notion as a tournament helmet offered by the German dealer Lennart Viebahn was variously damaged by numerous sword cuts and repaired with rivets and molten copper inserts. It had obviously taken quite a few knocks! Its value: around £48,000. However, big-league items tend to be rather more expensive. Swiss auctioneers Fischer, in Lucerne, have a reputation for offering exceptional pieces and a *Feldküriss* (three-quarter armour) dating from *c*.1535 etched by the famous Ambrose Gemlich made a deserving £152,000.

Van's the Man

Fiona Bruce has been the presenter on the *Antiques Roadshow* since 2008. She's the third front person I have worked with over many years on the show and has become an increasing devotee of antiques and art. It is not her first incarnation as a presenter on an art show: she originally worked on BBC2's *The Antiques Show*, which no doubt whetted her appetite for the *Antiques Roadshow* when Michael Aspel retired. Fiona has of course gone on to work with my fellow *Roadshow* specialist Philip Mould on the popular art sleuthing show, *Fake or Fortune*. Not surprising, then, that she has developed a bit of an eye for an interesting picture.

Imagine the scenario: a gentleman comes to a show with

an oil painting of a man's head bearing a label inscribed 'Van Dyck'. It's necessary to take such labels with a pinch of salt, mainly due to countless pictures being wrongly attributed over the centuries. Often they are copies of well-known originals. Father Jamie MacLeod, owner of the picture, had purchased it from a Cheshire antiques shop for just £400 but suspicions were aroused by specialist Philip (who is somewhat of a Van Dyck expert) and Fiona when they felt that certain aspects of the picture looked to be by the great man, particularly the way the tear ducts were executed – a trademark signature of a white dash.

After some exhaustive research and a thorough cutting back of 19th-century embellishment, the simpler and more sketchy result turned out to be an oil study for a now lost work executed in 1634, which was destroyed by the French in 1695. The head is one of a group of seven Brussels magistrates and was subsequently verified by Dr Christopher Brown, a leading authority on Van Dyck, as definitely the genuine article.

Father Jamie MacLeod, in a very magnanimous gesture, was immediately happy to offer it for sale to buy new church bells. Unfortunately, when it was offered for sale at Christie's it failed to find a buyer. The reasons for it not selling are unclear but picture buyers are sometimes a secretive set and perhaps all the pre-sale publicity over-exposed it; however, I'm sure this is not the last we'll hear of it.

Alter Ego

I've always fancied myself as a bit of a dandy. It's a rather idealised notion of living in romantic, gallant and more decadent times (totally mis-founded in reality) and living like a Cruikshank caricature, a Dick Wildfire-type Lothario brawling his way around Paris with his squire in tow, Wogdons (duelling pistols) at the ready, drunk on Madeira. In between times I could pop into the Louvre and flirt with a few more ladies from Parisian high society in the slightly edgy post-revolutionary atmosphere of the capital and probably end up the subject of a satirical print. Sounds good to me!

I have a small collection of 18th and early 19th-century caricatures. Apparently, the art form originates in the 16th-century pastime of *ritratti caricati*, the art of the 'loaded portrait'. The stylised, exaggerated and comical illustrative form of comment has a strong historical tradition in the pages of our printed media, going back to the late 18th- and early 19th-century 'golden age' of masters such as Thomas Rowlandson, James Gillray and George Cruikshank. Collecting such prints has long been the domain of the studious, well-heeled connoisseur and it's not difficult to see the attraction of this art form.

These 'cartoons' are often so loaded with double entendre and coarse wit that they serve as a perfect illustration

of political feeling, disenchantment and humorous comment on all sectors of society, but particularly royalty
and the upper classes. Many are wonderfully provocative,
cloaked with innuendo and sexual references about who
was in bed with whom, political megalomaniacs, unfair
taxes and the Prince Regent's expanding waistline. One
of my favourites is Gillray's famous cartoon of William
Pitt and Napoleon carving up a giant global pudding –
classic. These are historic documents in their own way
and an original Gillray of Pitt and Napoleon could cost
you £10,000.

So with the market buoyant and the scarcity of good, original prints always provoking healthy competition among

the cognoscenti of the genre, the re-distribution of a classic collection always brings a new set of values to serve as the next benchmark. Bloomsbury Auctions were able to offer one such collection, built over some 30 years by a British collector residing in America. Described by the *Antiques Trade Gazette* as a 'white glove' affair, no doubt with reference to the careful handling required, work by Thomas Rowlandson provided the highest prices of the day, including one of only three known copies of an album entitled *Comparative Anatomy: Resemblances Between the Countenances of Men and Beasts*. Dating from around 1822, it was replete with various pencil and ink drawings of anthropomorphic-type animals and humans – it realised £48,000. By far my choice of the sale was the wonderful 'Skating Dandies, shewing off', a print from the five-volume set of George Moutard Woodward's *Caricature Magazine, or Hudibrastic Mirror*. These realised £30,000.

Remember, this is quite a specialised market and while you may come across examples of such prints on your travels, most are later re-strikes and worth comparatively little. Alternatively, these can be an eminently accessible way to the subject matter and a very decorative statement on a well-placed 'print wall'.

Pigeon Fancier

Animals have played an important role throughout the history of warfare. The Dickin Medal was instituted in 1943 by the founder of the People's Dispensary for Sick Animals (PDSA) Maria Dickin as the animal equivalent of the Victoria Cross. Although it has been awarded on just 64 occasions, it comes up at auction relatively frequently. However, Bosleys auctioneers of Marlow recently offered a medal for a pigeon called Duke of Normandy. Bred in a loft in Frithville Gardens, Shepherds Bush, London, in 1941, he was distinguished by 'being the first bird to arrive with a message from Paratroops of 21st Army Group behind enemy lines on D Day 6th June 1944 while serving with the Allied Pigeon Service.' Despite terrible gales, explosions and bullets, Duke made it back to his loft in Shepherd's Bush from Sword Beach in 26 hours and 50 minutes with the momentous news of a successful invasion. The Duke's heroic medal made £8,000.

Favourite Finds

I never know what I might buy next. That's the problem with being an eclectic collector, a miscellaneous veteran and an inquisitive person. When I view an auction, walk around a fair or visit an antiques shop, I can be taken by just about anything that stirs my interest. Like most collectors, I need the object to speak to me. It doesn't always have to be a very involved conversation, sometimes just a passing comment that engages me in some way. It could be the craftsmanship, an event in history, sheer quirkiness, rarity, or even its size: I love surreal oversized things like giant shoes made for the windows of old cobblers' shops; or miniaturisation like an Indian grain of rice with 147 letters inscribed on it (I have one of those too). To be frank, every outing is an adventure because I have no idea what I might come home with next. Sometimes I'll buy something simply to turn a profit, which will then allow me to buy something else, and when I buy something more valuable it invariably goes straight on a shelf for my retirement fund, which is a euphemism for 'can't bear to part with it'!

The point of all this is to explain some of my favourite acquisitions this year – value not important!

1. A pretty spectacular early 19th-century reliquary case for St Concordius, devoid of all its bones but now

handsomely restocked with an interesting selection of 19th-century ex-anatomical human remains purchased, of all places, on eBay.

2. A 1955 Hofner Senator semi-acoustic guitar. I can never resist a vintage guitar. I now have two of this model but I can never resist a 'brunette' (the colour of the guitar).

3. A set of six wooden napkin rings fashioned from the salvaged teak of German ships scuttled at the Royal Navy base of Scapa Flow after the end of the First World War. Seventy-four ships of the German High Seas Fleet were impounded awaiting a decision by the Allies but, fearing that they would all be seized, Admiral Ludwig von Reuter ordered them all scuttled. Fifty-two sank, some were beached; many have been salvaged for scrap. Some still remain there. Among the rings is one made from the battleship *Prinzregent Luitpold*. It's a nice talking point when you ask the guests which ship of the German fleet they are representing.

4. A Napoleonic prisoner-of-war bone model in a bottle. This is one of my favourites and features a naively carved bonneted lady operating a complicated triple yarn winder in front of some stylised wooden trees. French prisoners from the Napoleonic wars fashioned

such items from leftover bones and sold them to prison visitors in order to buy the basics, such as food! This acquisition was a bargain that I spotted sleeping in an auction box and has been a welcome addition to my collection!

5. A lovely 18th-century glass tazza (comport) to complete my graduated stack of three and originally used to display jellies and syllabubs in the middle of a table. Of course, this is exactly what I use it for and it can hold a very majestic 30 jelly glasses without crowding!

6. A late 19th-century lightweight Thomas Turner twelve-bore box-lock shotgun, which I carry mostly for decoration when out on a country ramble (rather than calling it a shoot) – a marvellous piece of craftsmanship.

7. A brass cartridge case bearing a printed paper label reading: 'This cartridge case was picked up at Ladysmith during the siege, shipped from Durban by mail steamer "Scot", August 13th 1900.' An emotive little piece of history from the Second Boer War and the famous siege of Ladysmith.

Great Dane

If you were expecting a piece about a famous person of Danish origin then you are barking up the wrong tree. The Great Dane in this excerpt is a dog, and a courageous one at that! I previously mentioned the Dickin Medal and a gallant recipient called Duke – a pigeon no less (*see page 128*). Well, another gong awarded to courageous animals was the Blue Cross Medal. Originally founded in 1897 as Our Dumb Friends League, the organisation changed its name to Blue Cross in the 1950s. Wotton Auction Rooms were recently able to offer a Blue Cross medal, one with an interesting story and awarded to a Great Dane called Juliana.

So the story goes, Juliana extinguished an incendiary bomb in 1941 after it smashed through the roof of her owners' home. I'm not quite sure how she did this – the mind boggles. Apparently, Juliana also alerted the owners when fire engulfed the house and resultantly saved their lives. A watercolour picture of Juliana accompanied the medal, with her feats outlined on a brass plaque. Unfortunately, the story has a less happy ending because Juliana was apparently poisoned in 1946 after someone put poison through the letterbox – a sad conclusion to a gallant tale. Given the scarcity and story behind the medal the £60–80 estimate was soon surpassed and it sold for £1,100.

Hair Today Gone Tomorrow

Celebrity collectables are big business. There are plenty of companies, particularly in America, that specialise in selling limited editions of specially signed objects: baseballs, basketballs, autographed photographs, artefacts and hair – yes, hair. Let me explain.

I've always been interested in the hair of famous people (*see* 'Severed Head', *page 21*). Hair of all kinds, woven into bracelets and exquisite creations in memento mori, has always been a popular keepsake, a souvenir of a loved one or perhaps a famous person.

The following excerpt is taken from *Godey's Lady's Book*, an American monthly that contained poetry, practical projects, articles and illustrations. At its height, *c.*1860, circulation was over 150,000 a month.

> Hair is at once the most delicate and lasting of our materials, and survives us, like love. It is so light, so gentle, so escaping from the idea of death, that with a lock of hair belonging to a child or friend, we may almost look up to heaven and compare notes with the angelic nature – may almost say; 'I have a piece of thee here, not unworthy of thy being now'

Pertinent words, particularly in the Victorian period when death and infant mortality were so common. No wonder that there are so many mementoes containing hair in the form of brooches, pins, necklaces and bracelets, some entirely woven of human hair. This type of mourning jewellery is very collectable.

So, armed with an idea (albeit a strange one), I took to the internet to see whose hair was for sale. If the idea of putting a product code into your on-line basket seems more akin to buying groceries then think again. Buying antiques and collectables can be just the same, and I often push the boundaries of probability by trawling around the net to see how diverse and just how weird and wonderful it can possibly get. One gateway to hairy heaven is Paul Fraser Collectibles where you'll find a whole head of well-presented mounted melanin curiosities. Starting at an affordable £49.95 it seems you can own some pretty amazing strands of famous follicles; but here's the catch: when it comes to such luminaries as George Washington, Elvis, the Duke of Wellington and Baron von Richthofen, the crux is that you are only buying one strand. Enough for a talking point, you might argue, but savvy salesmanship if you happen to have bought a whole lock!

In fairness, you could buy a multi-celebrity hair selection for £450 or a multi-historic collection for £650 – even a whole lock of Nelson's hair for £15,000. But top of my tree for the overpriced lot is a pot of hair from Justin Bieber's 'famous' haircut (which was sold for charity) – a snip at a mere £35,000! Gulp!

If this is too much of a stretch financially, then don't desphair [*sic*], the 'layaway' plan is a payment system allowing you to pay in monthly instalments. Also on the site are Mahatma Gandhi's food bowl, fork and spoons. Truly historic items and no denying that, but at £75,000 your personal plan will set you back £4,166.66 per month for eighteen months. Sounds like I might have to start budgeting!

Amber Gambler

I've visited the Catherine Palace near St Petersburg in Russia on several occasions. Given its virtual destruction at the hands of the Nazis in the Second World War it's hard to imagine that what you see is not completely original. The so-called amber room is a major attraction and was constructed in the early 18th century in Prussia. It was later installed in the Catherine Palace as a gift from the Prussian King, Wilhelm III to Tsar Peter the Great and was added to by the Tsar. It was finished in 1755 and contained over six tons of amber backed with gold leaf and inlaid with

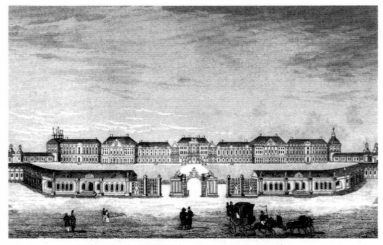

The Catherine Palace near St Petersburg

semi-precious stones. The room was often referred to as one of the 'wonders of the world'. You've perhaps realised that I'm talking about the original in the past tense – the Nazis looted the entire room and it has never been recovered.

The present room is an amazing reconstruction, just like the bulk of the palace, and was completed in 2003 after several decades of painstaking work. There is one original panel sited in the room, which came to light in 1997 via the family of a German soldier who claimed to have helped pack the amber room. However, despite extensive searches the whereabouts of the remainder are a complete enigma: perhaps still hidden; perhaps burnt or lost on a sunken ship. The most likely theory seems to be that it was lost in the fire that engulfed Königsberg Castle, when the German garrison surrendered to Soviet forces. Nobody seems to know its true fate.

However, its value would be beyond estimation – unlike an amazing amber chess board that came up for sale at Sotheby's. The board was attributed to a 17th-century maker, Georg Schreiber of Königsberg, a craftsman operating in a period often known as 'the golden age' for amber work. It came with an interesting provenance, apparently given by the Elector of Brandenburg, who controlled Russia, as a diplomatic gift to King James I. It then passed (by repute) to Charles I whereupon he bequeathed 'an amber games board', while on the scaffold, to William Juxon, Bishop of London. This can't be substantiated but this particular board descended through the Juxon family and thence to the Hesketh family in the 18th century, where it has remained ever since. Whatever the true story, it was enough to take the board to the dizzy heights of £500,000.

Ballet Buffet

You may have heard of a 19th-century ballet dancer by the name of Marie Taglioni. To be honest, I'm not a great fan of ballet and it wasn't until I noticed an interesting volume, *La Sulphide: Souvenir d'adieu de Marie Taglioni*, published in 1845, that had sold at Bonhams for £3,000, that I realised how important she was to the history of dance. The book, with six plates after Alfred Edward Chalon all marked 'proof', was printed to commemorate one of the last appearances on stage of a dancer renowned for her *en pointe* work and short skirt, which apparently caused quite a stir at the time. What attracted me to the story, was not so much the high price paid for a volume with no real precedent in the marketplace, but the fact that following her last appearance in Russia, several ardent fans were reported to have purchased her ballet shoes for 200 roubles in order that they could be cooked and eaten. I'm not sure what sauce they would have used as an accompaniment but that's definitely devotion for you!

Slice of Apple

Steve Jobs was the co-founder of Apple Inc. He is renowned as one of the greatest technical innovators of the 20th century, and is described in various sources as 'the master evangelist of the digital age', 'visionary', 'futurist' and 'design perfectionist'. He is regarded as a pioneer in the field of personal computing.

In 1976, Steve Wozniak, a friend and colleague of Jobs, created the first Apple computer – the Apple 1. Together with Ronald Wayne (who left shortly afterwards) they formed the company Apple Computer in the garage of Jobs' parents. The rest is highly convoluted but history nevertheless.

In the meantime, the computers have become highly important technological collectables and Team Breker Auctions of Cologne were recently able to offer an original working model of the Apple 1: 'no. 46' from the first batch of 50. Of the approximately 200 originally made, about 46 survive and there are only thought to be six working models left – this was one of them. Complete with circuit board signed by Wozniak and original accessories such as the tape player and keyboard, it was also thought to be the only one in its white cardboard box. Such was the anticipation of the sale that Team Breker even advertised it on an electronic billboard in Times Square. The original purchase price was $666.66. It was sold, on the internet, of course, to an Asian buyer for $650,000.

Haus Design

Christian Dell (1893–1974) was a German metalwork designer and silversmith. From 1922 to 1925 he worked as the foreman in the highly important and influential design school of the Bauhaus in Weimar. Afterwards he worked for the lamp and lighting manufacturers Gebr. Kaiser & Co. The company's 1936 catalogue contained Dell's classic design, the 6631 Luxus, now an iconic lamp among design aficionados.

Despite the plethora of archival material and artefacts generated by the Bauhaus, it's quite staggering when something hitherto undocumented surfaces. Such was the case with an electroplated three-piece nickel-silver 'mocha service' (for serving espresso-style coffee with milk) designed by Dell. Although a picture of Dell exists with a similar service – the whereabouts of which is unknown – this one is obviously one of a small stable of pieces that he executed at the Bauhaus. It has typical Bauhaus traits, particularly the solid semi-circular ebony handle on the milk jug. Nagel in Stuttgart offered the trio in their design sale and the resulting price was a strongly brewed £52,630.

Flag Day

María Eva Duarte de Perón, or Eva Perón (1919–1952) has an almost immortal or mythical status. The wife of the Argentine President, Juan Perón, and popularly known as Evita, she came from a humble background but won the hearts of the people of Argentina for her support of the poor and for her principled feminist ideals. She died of cancer aged just 33 and her body was embalmed by Doctor Pedro Ara, whose method of preservation involved replacing the blood with glycerine. A giant monument was proposed to display Evita's body to the public but after two years of building, Juan Perón was overthrown in a military coup. Evita's body disappeared for sixteen years and under the rule of the dictatorship it was illegal to even possess a photograph of the Peróns.

In 1971, it was revealed that she was in fact buried in a crypt in Milan under a different name and that the body had suffered some disfiguration due to poor handling. She was exhumed and transferred to Spain where the exiled Juan looked after her corpse and apparently kept it on a dais near the dining room table. When Juan returned in 1973 to take up the presidency for the third time, Evita's body was returned to Argentina. He died a year later and her body – after a brief period of display together – was buried in the family tomb in Buenos Aires. The tomb was built by a company that specialised in bank vaults and was made extremely secure for fear that her body might be stolen. But it was Juan's body that suffered the ignominious fate in 1987 of having the hands removed by chainsaw. They were ransomed for $8 million but not recovered. Various personal effects were also taken. The crime has never been solved.

It was after the coup in 1955 that a division of the military government known as the National Wealth Recovery Board auctioned off the Peróns' possessions. These included 65 cars. Another article that came under the hammer was a brooch in the form of the Argentine flag. It had belonged to Evita and was made by Van Cleef & Arpels in the mid-1940s. Constructed with the so-called 'mystery setting' invented by the company in 1935, the fluttering flag is mounted with a carpet of bevelled sapphires and diamonds with the central 'Sun of May', which represents the May 1810 election of Argentina's first colonial government, set with yellow diamonds in the centre.

The brooch first came back to the market in 1998 and made a remarkable $992,500 (inclusive of commission). Its recent reappearance at Christie's 'Magnificent Jewels' sale saw less fervour on the day when it sold for $461,000.

Watch This

The 1980s heralded a boom in vintage wristwatch collecting. Fuelled by the city bonus culture and buoyant economy, certain types of hitherto sidelined watches started to gain momentum. I've written several articles over the years on collecting watches for investment and it's always fascinating to see how the vagaries of the market play out. One of my personal favourites is the Rolex Daytona. Watches have also gained celebrity cachet and collectors attach great value to their film and showbiz connections. Sean Connery, as James Bond, in films such as *Dr. No* and *Goldfinger*, wore a Rolex Submariner, a brand that no doubt reinforced the image of a tough, all-action hero. Bond's character has also worn Omega and Seiko.

Rolex is a brand that has cemented the idea of quality in our psyche; a name founded on the idea of 'timeless luxury' and high-class advertising. It is one of the most valuable trademarks in the world.

To celebrate the 50th anniversary of its first chronograph, the Daytona, Christie's Geneva held a well-timed themed sale of 50 classic watches. Star of the auction was a 1969 black-dial 6263 'Paul Newman' model (more clever marketing!), one of few Daytona watches with a black dial and waterproof screw-down pushers. This early version, distinguished by the wording 'Rolex Cosmograph Oyster', rather than the modern 'Rolex Oyster Cosmograph', had apparently lain in stock for almost ten years, indicating that it wasn't the easiest watch to sell. In fact, only a dozen or so seem to have appeared on the market. In this case time was able to tell that perceptions and markets *do* change dramatically in the world of investment, fashion and collectables: the watch realised a tremendous £718,950! The sale raised $13.2 million – four times the estimate.

Plane as Day

Collecting antique tools is a popular pastime. I can hear people yawning at this point but tools are important and although I'm not a collector myself I do cherish a few of my great-grandfather's and grandfather's tools, namely a 19th-century saw, some rosewood spirit levels and a couple of woodworking planes.

My grandfather was a craftsman. He taught at Harrow School and one of my overriding memories of being a small boy is the smell of machine-tool suds in the workshops. He could make just about anything, from violins to steam-powered scale locomotives, and had several patents to his name. I like to think that I inherited some of his practical attributes and that's why I keep his tools. So whatever it is that fires one's habit, it's alright with me, and I hope that I can at least appreciate why people have a propensity to collect in one area, as opposed to another.

Woodworking planes come in a staggering variety of shapes and sizes. The most famous British manufacturer was T. Norris & Son of London. Founded in 1860, the firm produced a great number of planes and many of them are eminently collectable. Planes generally fall into two categories – bench and block. They are used for all manner of work, including reducing, smoothing, cutting decorative mouldings and making joints. Some are very specialist.

David Stanley Auctions are renowned for their specialist tool sales. Their auctions are vast, sometimes comprising 2,000 lots and several thousand items. They have lately been selling part of the extraordinary David R. Russell Collection. The collection, amassed over some 40 years, comprised over 2,000 woodworking tools ranging from the ancient up to the present day, of which over 1,500 are illustrated in a definitive catalogue. When they recently sold several instalments from the collection, planes were again high on the list of 'must-have' items and although Norris tools tend to form the mainstay of such sales, there were several others that did well. Apparently, the first American plane maker to stamp his work was an N. Potter, and a rare early 18th-century example made £5,500. A wonderful decorative brass-inlaid European coachbuilders plane made £3,800 but top of the tree were the Norrises with an A28 gunmetal chariot plane that realised £6,000 and a 28in (that's big!) A1 steel jointer that made a mighty £8,200. Next time you malign the boxes of rusty tools at your local auction, think again!

※ᢒᢗᢒ᠅ᢒ᠅

Chocoholic

Desperation. Pacification. Expectation.
Acclamation. Realization it's 'Fry's'.

In 1902, the famous Quaker confectionery company of J.S. Fry's launched a chocolate bar called 'Five Boys'. It cost 6d and the wrapper featured five images of a young boy pulling various facial expressions as his initially desperate countenance turns to pleasure at the realisation that he is about to partake in a bar of Fry's chocolate. The brand is remarkably nostalgic and renowned as one of the most famous advertising gimmicks in confectionery history.

So the story goes, the photographer used his son – Lindsay Poulton – as the model, and was paid a staggering £200 for the exclusive use of the images. Apparently, in

order to take an image for 'Desperation', a rag was soaked in the photographer's ammonia and placed around Lindsay's neck – this made him cry. I'm not quite so sure what modern conventions would make of such a practice, but it obviously worked. The 'Five Boys' bar was eventually discontinued in 1976 but has remained popular with collectors of ephemera and advertising material. Most sought after are the enamel advertising signs, of which there are several variations. Anthemion Auctions of Cardiff recently offered a version which sold for a very sweet £2,900.

Chinese Junk

As many are perhaps aware, the literal translation of Hong Kong is 'fragrant harbour'. The name possibly refers to the fact that fresh water from the Pearl River 'sweetened' the harbour waters, or alternatively, that incense factories north of Kowloon stored their aromatic products in Aberdeen Harbour. One thing is certain: *kong* means 'harbour' or 'inlet'. However, *hong* is also the word for 'a commercial establishment or house of foreign trade' (while a *hòhng* is literally a 'row'). Meanwhile, the *cohong*, also known as *cong-hong* or *hong*, were the guild of Chinese merchants officially sanctioned by central government, up until the first Opium War (1839–42), to trade at Guangzhou (Canton) with Western merchants.

A trading system was in place by the mid-17th century, and by the 1740s foreign ships would come under the jurisdiction of an appointed *hong* merchant. These officials were responsible to the government for tax collection and ensuring that the foreigners behaved properly. When Guangzhou (75 miles north of Hong Kong on the Pearl River) was the only port open to foreign trade, the hong merchants were the only people allowed to sell tea and silk to Western traders, and wielded much power. This was known as the 'Canton System' and lasted from around 1700 to 1842. The foreign traders were kept to their waterfront factories – the *hongs* – where they were permitted to trade with the *gong-hang*, a consortium of hong merchants who effectively fixed all the prices.

Depictions of this trading history are much sought after and the Chinese responded to demand from traders for souvenirs of their visits by producing detailed paintings and finely decorated porcelain with views of the foreign hongs, flags flying and ships laid at anchor in the harbour.

A wonderful large (16in) 18th-century example of a Chinese porcelain 'mandarin palette' punchbowl, circa 1785, was offered by Wotton Auctions. Decorated with a wonderful scene of the Swedish, British and Dutch hongs and a selection of small vessels in the foreground, it sold for £37,000 – not an abnormal price in this strong area of history.

We Are Sailing

Clipper cards, or sailing cards as they are also known, were an advertising medium used in 19th-century America. The companies who owned the fast, streamlined clipper ships plying their trade out of ports such as San Francisco and Boston vied for freight business and passengers by issuing colourful lithographic cards extolling the virtues of their vessels: 'The Famous Extreme Clipper – *Rattler*' or such like. The ships to which they pertained were built between 1845 and 1855 and sacrificed cargo space for greater speed – hence the name *extreme* clipper. Medium clippers had greater stowage and 'good sailing qualities' but were ultimately slower. At the height of the California Gold Rush (1848–52) competition out of New York and Boston was intense and it was common to see cards with phrases such as 'current rates and no deception'. Sailing cards with Civil War imagery are very popular among collectors with ships sporting rousing names such as *Volunteer*.

The market is naturally strongest in America and cards can quite easily cost several hundred dollars each. A collection offered by PBA Galleries in San Francisco created great interest, particularly one card for the 'First Class Clipper' *Fanny S. Perley* bound for San Francisco. Dating from around 1860, it made $8,000.

❧❧❧

The Price of Freedom

I have a dream that my four little children
will one day live in a nation where they will
not be judged by the color of their skin
but by the content of their character.
I have a dream today!
—MARTIN LUTHER KING JR

Maude Ballou worked as Martin Luther King's personal secretary from 1955 to 1960. During that time Maude was working at the forefront of the civil rights movement as both King's friend and confidante, and she collected many personal and historical letters. Maude, now in her late 80s, made the decision to sell the archive, a move which would help to benefit an education fund at the Alabama State

University. However, in 2011, King's estate sued her son, Howard Ballou, to take possession of the items – but the courts ruled in favour of Ballou.

Of the several interesting lots offered for sale, a set of six handwritten notes dating from 1959, to inform his congregation that he would be leaving the Dexter Avenue Baptist Church, raised £31,500. Two letters sent to Maude from King's visit to India in 1959 made $18,750 and $18,000. The star lot – a typed final page of the iconic 'I have a dream' speech – was actually withdrawn 'pending further research', maybe to surface at another time? However, one item Maude was unable to part with was a copy of King's book *Stride Toward Freedom* with the inscription:

> To my secretary Maude Ballou, in appreciation for your good will, your devotion to your work, and your willingness to sacrifice beyond the call of duty in assisting me to achieve the ideals of freedom and human dignity for our people,
>
> [signed] Martin

Priceless!

Further to that archive, Heritage auctions of New York also sold a 1957 copy of *Time* magazine signed by King for $6,500. Emotive stuff!

The Master

Juan Manuel Fangio (1911–1995) was an Argentinian racing driver who dominated the first ten years of Formula 1 by winning the drivers' world championship no less than five times. His amazing career initially escalated in a new post-war generation of Mercedes-Benz cars that took the world of racing by storm. Pre-war, the Germans had dominated the track but during this period they remained absent, for obvious reasons.

The governing body of the sport launched its new Grand Prix regulations in 1954 and stipulated that engines should be no more than 2.5 litres and without superchargers. Mercedes missed the first two races of the new season but staged a momentous comeback with their 'slipper-bodied' straight-8 W196 model, a car with many technical innovations such as fuel injection, tubular lightweight chassis and inboard mounted brakes. Its debut at the French Grand Prix saw Fangio and his teammate Karl Kling take first and second place, trumpeting the return of Mercedes across the world. The car that Fangio was driving was chassis number 00006/54 – a legendary car.

Although other legendary cars have been sold for enormous sums of money, including the recent private sale of a 1963 Ferrari 250 GTO for $52 million, the sale of '00006' by Bonhams Auctioneers constituted the most expensive car sold at auction to date. Previously in the collection of the National Motor Museum in Beaulieu, it was sold in 1973; 00006 then went through the hands of several private collectors in the intervening years before being offered by Bonhams in their historic sale. The car realised a commission-inclusive £19.6 million.

Sadly, there is a sombre footnote to the story of Mercedes' on-track success. It was relatively short-lived due to a horrendous accident that officially killed 83 people at the 1955 Le Mans motor race (the number is disputed). A Mercedes-Benz 300SLR crashed into the crowd after a braking accident involving Jaguar and Austin-Healey. Fangio was on the track but it was his teammate Pierre Levegh who hit the Healey, sending his disintegrating airborne car into the crowd, causing a deadly shower of debris and burning Elektron magnesium alloy body parts. Levegh and 82 spectators died, with 120 injured; Mercedes withdrew from competition racing altogether, only returning in 1987. This was the worst motor racing accident in history and led to a root and branch review of crowd safety issues.

Pooled Resources

In many areas of collecting, bubbles tend to form, prices hit a peak and then they often recede. This can depend on many different factors, particularly the economic climate. Over several decades, I've seen many genres have their day. If you're a specialist dealer, it's often a case of making hay while the sun shines then knowing when to get out before the bubble bursts. It's the same in any investment-oriented business that has that unpredictable element of human emotion somewhere in the equation.

Poole pottery was such a market and some ten years ago prices were very high for the superlative pieces. Back in 2004 Cottees of Wareham sold a vase painted by Anne Hansard for £16,000. It's a record that's unlikely to be broken.

The factory, established in 1898, was originally known as Carter's Industrial Tile Manufactory and marked its early wares with a 'Carter Stabler Adams' impression, after founders and designers Jesse Carter, Harold and Phoebie Stabler and John and Truda Adams (née Carter). They collaborated to produce their distinctive range of Art Deco pottery. The early clay was orange, giving the bases of their pieces a distinguishing colour; however, this deposit dwindled and they switched to a light clay and coloured the bases with an orange slip.

The factory's trademark ranges include the 'Twintone' two-colour wares, now popular with budget-end collectors, and the later very vibrant and highly collected 'Delphis' and 'Aegean' introduced in 1963 and 1970 respectively. Large pieces by designers such as Tony Morris can fetch thousands of pounds and are very much favoured by contemporary interior designers.

The factory on Poole Quayside closed in 2006 with debts of over £1 million but the brand has been revitalised by Lifestyle Group Ltd, who have reopened in Poole. This rebirth has also seen a marked rise in interest in the pottery and a good vase painted by Truda Carter was recently sold by Shapes of Edinburgh for a robust £7,000.

Napoleon's Noisette

The idea of Napoleon drinking a Costa coffee might seem a little odd but that's the image that was conjured up in my head when I saw that Napoleon's coffee table had recently sold at auction. The early 19th-century table was one of a 'nesting' set of four 'quartet' tables and bore a silver plaque engraved with the words:

CETTE PETITE TABLE PROVIENT DU MOBILIER DE
L'EMPEREUR NAPOLEON ET ETAIT PORTEE CHACQUE
JOUR SUR LA TERRASSE A St HELENE OU S.M. PRENAIT
LE CAFE.

Lyon and Turnbull Auctioneers hedged their bets on the estimate, giving it a low £300 with the suggestion that it resembled one in the well-known deathbed painting of Napoleon. I quickly spotted it in Carl Von Steuben's famous depiction of the scene and the table is definitely part of a 'quartet'. Longwood House on St Helena where Napoleon was exiled in 1815 still has another table from the set

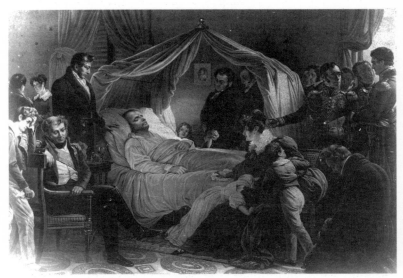

Napoleon on his deathbed, as depicted by Carl
Von Steuben. His coffee table is just nestling on the left

although I'm not sure whether they've ever been 'matched up'. Whatever the general doubts, all of this seemed quite adequate provenance for the buyer who was prepared to pay £2,100 to secure it. Even as part of a set I think it was probably not bad value for the Emperor's coffee table ... make mine an Americano.

Completely Jaded

Our celestial empire possesses all things in prolific abundance and lacks no products within its own borders. There is therefore no need to import the manufactures of outside barbarians.
—Chien-lung (1711–1799), Emperor of China
(letter to King George III of England)

I love my work. Never a day seems to pass when I'm not surprised or enthralled; rarely a day passes when I don't learn something or find myself intrigued. Sometimes, I'm actually stuck for words. So it was the other day when I was handed an Imperial jade bowl (yes another jade story) undoubtedly commissioned by the Qianlong Emperor himself. Unfortunately, you will have to buy the next *Almanac* to find out its fate but at this point I can tell you that I am pretty excited about it.

Someone else who was undoubtedly pretty excited was the purchaser of a plain celadon coloured jade bowl they found in a charity sale for 50 pence. Canterbury Auction Galleries were concerned that the Qianlong four-character mark had been added later, which is not uncommon. However, buyers thought otherwise on the day and it sailed off to a mighty £15,500. A fairly hefty profit margin, even after the auctioneer's commission.

Pearl Jam

*All art is autobiographical. The pearl
is the oyster's autobiography.*
—FEDERICO FELLINI

Pearls are one of those marvellous wonders of nature. Their enigmatic origins and the mysterious nature of their creation have captivated people throughout history, adding to their decorative allure with mythical associations. Pearls can be formed inside any mollusc but are generally associated with oysters. Their formation is triggered by the intrusion of a parasite into the mollusc, and they range in colour from purest white to pink, yellow and even black; the size can also vary.

Oysters have been harvested for their precious inclusions for over 3,000 years and the Persian Gulf was once one of the world's main sources of this much-cherished gem of the seas. Natural pearls are relatively rare in terms of their ratio of occurrence and as many as 2,000 shells might have to be opened to find one good pearl. 'Oriental' pearls were in high demand over the centuries, revered and used in profusion as a show of status in royal regalia through to the long sautoirs of the flapper girls of the 1920s. However, by the 1930s, the market for natural pearls had started to fall into decline. The advent of mass-produced cultured pearls, whereby the natural process of pearls accidentally forming in an oyster was triggered by the manual insertion of a parasite, also distorted the market.

Despite these historical changes, recent years have seen a big renaissance in pearl interest and the price of natural examples has risen enormously. The world's largest pearl is a very ugly monster weighing in at 14lbs and was discovered in the Philippines in 1939 inside a giant clam. It's called the pearl of Lao Tzu. It has no lustre like conventional pearls as clams don't produce nacre, the substance that makes pearls glisten. However, it still has a value of around £2 million, due to its sheer size. Notably high prices in recent times include the $3.3 million paid for a row of 38 graduated grey pearls from the late Viscountess Cowdray, Lady Pearson (1860–1932), sold by Christie's.

Even more incredible was the sale of a single natural pearl by the auctioneers Woolley and Wallis of Salisbury. A client arriving with a pair of earrings each hung with a single large pearl was amazed to be told that one of the pearls was natural. After some exhaustive testing and confirmation by several institutions it was confirmed as a pearl of exceptional size and rarity, weighing 132.59 grains. Measuring a maximum 17.4mm, the auctioneers thought that it might be the biggest natural pearl to ever be sold at auction. Bidding on the day was extremely fierce and it was finally knocked down for a commission-inclusive £811,600.

So, the Victoria & Albert museum's timely exhibition entitled 'Pearls' seemed very apt considering the heightened interest. I enjoyed the exhibition greatly, although, like many such events, it did seem to a get a little over-crowded. What made this exhibition difficult was the fact that many of the exhibits were displayed in converted 19th-century safes. The idea, although aesthetically pleasing, made it nigh-on impossible for more than two people at any one time to peep through the armoured glass windows of these suggestively secure display cases. I did, on several occasions, monopolise some of the 'safes' and was particularly moved by one single exhibit – the pearl drop earring worn by Charles I to his execution in 1649. This I gazed upon for some time, much to the annoyance of other gallery goers.

Angels of Death

Sometimes, I look at the huge amounts of money that need to be raised to save works of art and objects for the nation and fleetingly wonder whether we can possibly justify them. It's not a thought that usually lasts very long, particularly when it's something uniquely valuable to our heritage, but it often seems like an arduous struggle for some of the institutions that have to stare month after month at their electronic fundraising 'thermometers' hoping that they will get ever warmer. Just a few million? Well that can't be that much, surely, to save something as important as the bronze angels that were cast to embellish the tomb of Sir Cardinal Wolsey?

These are known as the Wolsey Angels, and this is the kind of appeal that doesn't tend to hit the headlines, but it's a remarkable tale of four bronzes commissioned in 1524 from the Renaissance Florentine sculptor Benedetto da Rovezzano to adorn the tomb of Henry VIII's chief advisor and ill-fated Cardinal. Working under Wolsey's patronage, Benedetto was a contemporary of Michelangelo and his patron's plan to mount these on his tomb as a symbol of wealth and status unfortunately never came to fruition. Henry had for some time been trying to annul his marriage to Catherine of Aragon but Wolsey had been having no success in trying to persuade the Pope to agree. His career suffered as a result and he passed away in 1530 before his tomb was completed.

Typically, it seems, Henry's behaviour was less than respectful and he took the four bronze angels and other elements of Wolsey's tomb for use on his own tomb, while also employing Benedetto to work on an even more lavish shrine of interment. Henry too died before it was completed and his children failed to fulfil their obligation to finish it. The angels were never used.

Henry's tomb was later moved to St George's Chapel in Windsor by Elizabeth I but the turmoil of the Civil War led to various elements being sold off – quite incredible really. The black stone sarcophagus survived and now contains the body of Admiral Lord Nelson which is interred in the crypt of St Paul's Cathedral. With most of the tomb's components lost to history, it was in 1994 that two bronzes appeared at a sale in Sotheby's, catalogued as 'a pair of large bronze angels in the Renaissance style'. An Italian art historian, Francesco Caglioti, did finally attribute them to Benedetto, which led to the discovery in 2008 of the other two angels at Harrowden Hall in Northamptonshire. Apparently, the Sotheby's pair had been stolen in 1988, prior to which all four had stood above the gates.

It's an incredible tale and one that now needs £5 million to resolve by uniting them once again and keeping them together for the nation. At the time of writing the thermometer is looking pretty lukewarm at £100,275 but I'm hoping that they will have managed to hit the target by the date of publication.

Wolsey's angels guarding the gates of
Harrowden Hall in the early 20th century

Keeping Up With the Joneses

Traditionally, watercolours never realise as much as oil paintings. However, despite the often reported poor state of the Victorian picture market, there are always exceptions to the general rule.

The major players in the Pre-Raphaelite market are well known. Andrew Lloyd-Webber and Isabel Goldsmith have tangled on numerous occasions in pursuit of the best of the genre. The appearance of 'Love Among the Ruins' by Edward Coley Burne-Jones (1833–1898) was one of those rare occasions when a work of such importance and still in private hands actually comes to the saleroom, and competition on the day was extremely fierce for a work that is considered by many to be the artist's most important picture.

Completed in 1873, the work is intensely symbolic as it depicts the love of Burne-Jones for Maria Zambaco, the woman for whom he left his wife. Typically, their relationship was deemed scandalous and the picture is poignant in that it shows the couple comforting each other surrounded by the thorns of society's hostility in the form of an encroaching dog rose. What is more emotive is that Jones thought the picture had actually been destroyed at one point due to an accident in Paris when a photographer covered the picture in albumen (used in

19th-century photographic processes). Luckily, the damage was not too extensive but the head of the woman required repainting and this was also the subject of some conjecture, eventually settled by scientific means. Had the head been repainted by his assistant, Charles Fairfax Murray, the picture would have certainly suffered the financial consequences.

Conjecture about its potential value was rife. The previous record for a Burne-Jones was £1 million and the estimate for 'Love Among the Ruins' seemed punchy at £3–5 million. However, good Pre-Raphaelite works have apparently been changing hands privately for far in excess of this amount and new bidding blood in the marketplace from foreign climes (probably China and Russia) meant that this powerful work was always going to transcend the 'Victorian' label that is so often added in a rather derogatory way. Pundits were hardly wrong as it sailed to £13.2 million, making it a very expensive watercolour indeed. Whether or not this is an indicator of a general rise in the medium is doubtful but it certainly cements the reputation of Burne-Jones as one of the great Pre-Raphaelite artists.

Bank On It

Graffiti is nothing new. I'm a bit of a graffiti addict, and in its own way (I don't condone vandalism) it can add a tantalising layer of history to certain edifices. The popular impression of graffiti is that it lowers the tone, causing degradation while emphasising social problems in an area. This is often true but visit any ancient site and you are likely to find some – perhaps several centuries' worth of names and epigraphs carved and scratched into the walls. Whether it's period to the building itself – perhaps a disenchanted stonemason chiselling something rude about his boss – or an early 19th-century Grand Tourist leaving his flamboyant cartouche on the side of a temple in Egypt, there's plenty of information and interest to be gleaned from some of this antique 'tagging'.

Several examples of my favourite pieces come from Pompeii, the once-thriving city entombed in the ash of Mount Vesuvius' eruption in AD79. The graffiti stands testament to the vibrancy of this great Roman city but is also an earthy insight into the everyday facets of life in what was obviously a gritty place to live. Some of the pieces are far too rude to be printed here but I can't resist just putting a few of the less risqué ones down on paper.

Peristyle of the Tavern of Verecundus: Restitutus says:

'Restituta, take off your tunic, please, and show us your hairy privates'.

In the basilica: No young buck is complete until he has fallen in love.

Bar of Astylus and Pardalus: Lovers are like bees in that they live a honeyed life.

House of Caecilius Iucundus: Whoever loves, let him flourish. Let him perish who knows not love. Let him perish twice over whoever forbids love.

Atrium of the House of Pinarius: If anyone does not believe in Venus, they should gaze at my girlfriend.

In the basilica: O walls, you have held up so much tedious graffiti that I am amazed that you have not already collapsed in ruins.

Some of the greatest names in history have left their mark upon the most important edifices in the world. Christopher Wren was obviously unabashed about carving his initials into Stonehenge. Indeed, one of the sarsens has disappeared because people hired hammers and chipped pieces from it to keep as souvenirs!

So, the idea of graffiti being of monetary value seems odd, does it not? Modern graffiti, or 'street art', is now regarded as an art form in its own right and here's where we diverge from the idea of writing your name on the side of a tube train with a can of spray paint into a world of renowned and often highly witty stylised artists. There are even dotcom companies that will custom produce 'street art' for you.

Making the transition between street artist and credible mainstream artist is probably not on the agenda of most graffiti artists, but some have inadvertently made that leap – big time! The whole point of graffiti, particularly the 20th-century genre, is often subversive and political. Some of the greatest proponents, such as the late Keith Haring, 'Sever' and 'Inkie' had notorious reputations as street artists and social activists before their work became internationally acclaimed. Haring's 'Radiant Baby' is an iconic symbol and his distinctive line-drawn imagery with its often overtly religious connotations spawned countless copy-cats.

Of course, no piece on graffiti would be complete without mentioning Banksy. By the time you read this, the *Antiques Roadshow* will have aired its first major piece by the Bristol-based artist (Bristol also being the production base of the *Roadshow*) and no doubt more of Banksy's works will have realised large amounts at auction. Banksy's irreverent style is undoubtedly the key to his success. His anonymity is also a clever factor which heightens the enigma that surrounds him. Add to this that Banksy draws inspiration from other successful street artists, while others also copy him, and that there always seems to be some kind of controversy surrounding both him and his art ... perfect advertising! Of course, some critics say that his work is vandalism and appeals to the lowest common denominator but there is no denying his wit, even if you don't like the art. Every time a new Banksy appears it seems that someone removes a large section of wall without permission and the owner-ship issues begin. It's also impossible to enter a card shop without his images jumping out from the racks. 'Kissing Coppers' is a favourite, an infamous work spray-painted on to the wall of the Prince Albert pub in Brighton and later removed. It's an iconic work and recently sold for £345,000 in New York.

High prices for Banksy's works include $1,870,000 paid for the canvas 'Keep It Spotless' and $658,000 for 'Rude Lord', to name but two. However – and this is a strange idiosyncrasy of his work – he effectively gives a great deal of it away by executing it in public places. One recent stunt, during a month-long residency in New York, involved an unmarked market stall which he set up in Central Park selling small signed original works for $60 (£38) each. Of course, few people would have believed they were real. Apparently he sold around eight, making the total tak-ings for the day $420 (one lady negotiated a discount). The actual value of the pictures is thought to be around

$20,000 each. I wonder, if I had been there, would I have bought one?

Bombing Mission

It's hard to imagine the fear that the sight of a Zeppelin airship would have struck into the hearts of the civilian population of Britain during the First World War. These huge, rigid flying machines were used quite effectively by the Germans to intimidate the general population over a series of fifty-one missions, which resulted in the deaths of over 550 civilians. The bombing was fairly indiscriminate because the Zeppelins were often hampered by poor night-time navigation. Adverse weather conditions also made missions highly risky and about 35 per cent of the Zeppelins were lost as a result of being either shot down or intercepted.

Although the Kaiser had approved the bombing raids, crews were instructed not to bomb London or historic buildings. Using an inaccurate system of dead reckoning and poor radio direction finding systems, bombs were literally just dropped overboard; so, despite the Kaiser's decree, accurate targeting of military installations was essentially impossible. But the raids were very detrimental to public morale and, as a result, a government inquiry was held. This proved highly influential in the creation of the Royal Air Force.

As British defences improved, bombing missions by Zeppelins were gradually replaced by those of aeroplanes. The huge Gotha biplane bombers could fly high and out of the range of the British fighters and they in turn killed over 830 people. Raids are commemorated by plaques in various places and I remember being rather fascinated as a boy when I found that several holes in one of the bronze lions flanking Cleopatra's Needle on the Thames Embankment had been made by a bomb dropped in 1917 on the first Gotha night raid.

Zeppelins are named after Count Ferdinand von Zeppelin. His interest in rigid airships, as opposed to much smaller 'frameless' dirigibles, began around 1874. By 1895 the Germans had patented their 'Zeppelin' design and the Americans followed suit a few years later with their version of a large rigid airship. By 1910 the Deutsche Luftschiffahrts-AG began the first commercial passenger flights, carrying some 10,000 passengers prior to the beginning of the First World War. However, the conflict caused a hiatus in production as the Treaty of Versailles forbade the Germans to continue with the production of large airships. The golden age of airship production and travel was in the 1920s and 30s; it was in this period that the famous LZ 127 *Graf Zeppelin,* LZ129 *Hindenburg* and LZ 130 *Graf Zeppelin II* plied the inter-continental routes from Germany to America and Brazil.

The Empire State building in New York is topped with a pylon, partly to make it the tallest building at the time, but also as an airship mooring point. It was only used once: not only was the sheer height impractical but the wind speeds were far too dangerous to moor large crafts. The demise of the great airships came about for various reasons. Firstly, Hitler used them as a propaganda tool, making sure that giant swastikas were emblazoned on the tail fins; the aerial presence of such an awe-inspiring machine was used with great effect at Nazi rallies and official functions but it also served to alienate and intimidate foreigners who found the symbolism threatening. Also, although inert helium was available, the Americans controlled its production and would not export it, forcing the Germans to continue using highly flammable hydrogen. The *Hindenburg* disaster in 1937 was a stark reminder of the volatile nature of hydrogen-filled airships and echoed the sad tragedy of the British airship R101 which crashed in 1930.

Airship material is highly collectable. Everything from lightweight cutlery to mangled pieces of duralumin alloy framing, crash mail and ephemera always garner interest. One area of rarity is the field of airship munitions. With just over 50 missions flown, such items are scarce, and so Wallis & Wallis's sale of part one of the David Kirch collection of airship memorabilia garnered great enthusiasm from bidders around the globe. Two bombs that had actually been dropped but (obviously) failed to detonate did well. An incendiary bomb that resembled a rather large wasp's nest made £2,600 and a 220lb naval aerial bomb realised £1,300. A pair of napkin rings made from Zeppelin wreckage and bearing an inscription made £300.

Pithy Stuff

I must have seen hundreds of pith helmets during my career. If anything symbolises our colonial past it must be this hat, a lightweight item of headgear sometimes called a safari helmet or sola topee and fashioned from either cork or pith from the sola plant. Covered in cloth, it was the favourite sun hat of the military, explorers, officials and plantation owners and became commonly known as the Foreign Service Helmet. Various styles evolved over a long period, building on variations of similar-looking helmets used at home by the military and police, as well as familiar-looking varieties used by foreign forces. Perhaps the most stereotypical

Sir Henry Morton Stanley, explorer, in pith helmet

vision of a pith-helmeted British trooper stems from our filmic experience of Michael Caine and Stanley Baker battling Zulus at Rorke's Drift.

Typically, they sell for very little. Military examples with regimental badges and perhaps topped-off with a fancy metal 'spike' might make £200–300 but generally they can be purchased for £30–40 at auction. No surprise then, that a Boer War example offered by Boulton & Cooper Auctioneers of Malton, in its black japanned tin transit case, came with exactly that estimate. However, this one had a rather interesting service history, having belonged to Major General Cuthbert (1861–1931) of the Scots Guards. His long career had taken him to the Sudan in 1885, South Africa from 1899 to 1902 and through the First World War. Interest in the lot pushed it to a pithy £5,400. Possibly the most expensive pith helmet ever!

Calculated Risk

Some of the 'mondo' numbers littered throughout this book can seem rather incomprehensible to those of us on more mediocre incomes and I'm sure that those in a position to spend such large amounts must often find themselves reaching for the calculator on their smartphones as the noughts pile up in various foreign currencies.

One calculator that wouldn't be able to deal with such large numbers is a little mechanical device known as the Arithomètre. Made by French mathematician and inventor

Charles Xavier Thomas (1785–1870), he served in the French army and founded several successful insurance companies, which allowed him to use the profits to finance his inventions. He launched his first calculator in around 1820 and the Arithomètre was the first such machine to be produced en masse as a numbered series. It's thought that as many as 5,000 were produced, although very few seem to have survived. Capable of performing several basic calculations, they are a favourite among scientific aficionados and collectors of such early devices.

Auction Team Breker of Cologne recently offered a good example in a brass and tortoiseshell case, given by Thomas to his future sister-in-law and inscribed to 'Mademoiselle de Renaud' (albeit misspelt from Reynaud) and numbered No. 541. It realised an impressive £166,665 and I'm sure many more jokes about calculations were likely to have been made on the day!

Cracking Lot

Nut crackers come in all shapes and sizes. I have several novelty examples that come out at Christmas, although having a wife who is highly allergic to nuts means that they often seem to be used more for festive decorative purposes than for serious snacking! I'm particularly fond of early boxwood 'lever' crackers dating from the 16th and 17th centuries. They gain a lovely smooth patina and are very characterful. The Leavenworth Nutcracker Museum in Washington State is famous for its collection of over 6,000 assorted examples dating from ancient to modern times.

Collectors of such items can often be found congregating at folk art and oak sales where a clever bit of marketing on the part of the auctioneer can seamlessly blend the allure of country furniture, treen, tole, fireside implements and goffering irons into a desirable 'look'. Indeed, many of the objects and furniture are highly desirable and not quite as unfashionable as the press would lead us to believe.

One cracking example of how rarity triumphs in such a market was the sale of a superb Charles II screw-action nutcracker at Bonhams. This form, which historically comes in several shapes and sizes, comprises a chip-carved sphere with a screw and decorative finial and had just about everything that any serious collector could desire. Dated objects always carry a premium and the 1664 inscribed on this one might not have been the earliest known example – Christie's sold an example in 1998 dated 1631 and Dreweatts had marginally pipped them on the date with one dated 1625 (which realised a hefty £9,000) but together with the rare inscription 'AS GOD HATH: A:

APPOINTED: SO: I: M : AM: CONTENTED' and a paper label inside dated 1956 stating that it was purchased for £7, it found no trouble making an all-inclusive £8,750! Not one to be put in the Christmas nut dish.

Good Sir Toby

I'm not really a big fan of Toby jugs. I suppose it stems from the countless poorly made cottage-style jovial-looking portly pipe-holding examples that I have had to deal with over the years – generally of very little value. However, their origins are quite interesting and the early examples dating from the mid-18th century are far more attractive and indeed far more collectable.

Often modelled on important people, salt-glaze and creamware Toby jugs were first made in England in the Staffordshire region and typically have tricorn hats with lids that form the crown of the hat. There have been various ideas put forward for the origins of the name. Some say it comes from Shakespeare's Sir Toby Belch in *Twelfth Night*. With the jugs also known as Philpots or Fillpots, an infamous 18th-century Yorkshire drinker called Henry Elwes or 'Toby Philpot', who was immortalised in a folk song called the 'Brown Jug', likewise lays claim to the Toby jug name.

Many examples are attributed to the famous Wood family of Staffordshire potters, particularly Ralph Wood (1715–1772), or are termed 'Ralph Wood' style, but these are just one of the many different objects that the Woods manufactured from their Burslem factory.

Despite the English ceramics market being at a low ebb in recent years, it appears that demand is always good for the best examples and having scouted around for the top achievers this year, the tricorn hat (rather than crown) goes to Woolley & Wallis Auctioneers for an unusual 'Step' Toby (that is, with a 'stepped' underbase) which had come from the collection of Lord Mackintosh of Halifax. It sold to an Australian bidder for £4,400.

⁂

The Yves of Something Big

A few years ago I wrote a report on the Christie's sale of Yves Saint Laurent's amazing art collection in Paris. Among the stunning selection of objects and furniture were two bronzes that caused an international incident at the time and looked very likely to affect Christie's transition into and position in the Asian markets, namely China. The reason for the problem was that among Yves' possessions were two bronze heads from the Haiyantang Zodiac water clock at the Old Summer Palace near Beijing.

The rat and the rabbit were two of twelve bronze heads supposedly designed by the Jesuit missionary Giuseppe Castiglione (1688–1766) and as such are regarded as important transitional Western/Oriental pieces. However, they were looted along with around a million other treasures when British and French forces sacked and destroyed the Summer Palace in 1860. The heads have become symbolic of the humiliation bestowed on the Chinese by this event and as such became pawns in a major diplomatic row. Although

The Hall of Calm Seas with the Zodiac water clock fountain

the two bronzes were acquired legally by Yves in the 1970s, tension rose over the decades as the Chinese tried to repatriate as many heads as possible. The whereabouts of five is still unknown but when these two were offered by Christie's the bidding soon rose to £25.4 million. The purchaser, Cai Mingchao, then refused to pay for them as a 'patriotic act of protest'. The future of Christie's in China had already been threatened by the Chinese State Administration of Cultural Heritage prior to the sale. Afterwards, Pierre Bergé, Yves' partner, was reported to have offered the bronzes to the Chinese people for nothing if China freed Tibet. Touché, you might think.

However, Bergé later sold the bronze heads to François-Henri Pinault (the Pinault family own Christie's), who has since presented them to the Chinese people amid expressions of 'high praise' from the Chinese government. What is certain is that this magnanimous gesture has certainly helped oil the wheels of Christie's business operations in China – an ever-expanding market buoyed by numerous billionaire collectors keen to repatriate China's stolen heritage. Smart move!

Cat Tales

*Authors like cats because they are such
quiet, lovable, wise creatures, and cats
like authors for the same reasons*
—ROBERTSON DAVIES

If I've heard the tale once I've heard it a hundred times: 'it was broken by the cat' or 'the cat knocked it off; we couldn't believe it wasn't damaged!' One Chinese vase that sold in 2013 for £2.6 million had apparently been subjected to the same treatment by a careless moggy weaving along a windowsill; luckily it wasn't broken. Having been the owner of a very characterful cat for some years myself, I don't ever recollect him knocking anything off accidentally, although he does have a habit of playfully flicking jewellery off the dressing table – on purpose!

Armed with several of these apocryphal tales I suggested that he be incorporated into the new title sequence for the next series of the *Antiques Roadshow*, which if I judge this correctly, means that Minou (French for 'pussy') should be quite well known by now as he artfully weaves his way through a selection of Grand Tour bronzes on a typical autumn's Sunday evening viewing schedule. Hopefully the fame won't go to his head but he might just about get away with having his own Twitter account. There's nothing like keeping it in the family!

Hotel Art

I had a friend some years ago who had a wonderful sideline selling art to hotel chains. He would pop over to China armed with a few auction catalogues and visit towns where artists vie, side by side in their little kiosks, to 'knock out' very faithful, well-executed copies of just about any type of picture you can imagine. So, after circling a few Old Masters and placing his order he would simply wait, amply entertained in the best restaurant in town (Pizza Hut), for the container to arrive at the docks. They really were actually rather good.

Most of the hotels I stay in tend to be of the 'Express' type. Although most hotel rooms seem to have a picture or two these days, they are often strictly limited to *not* strictly limited editions of rather wishy-washy prints. However, the art obviously varies depending on the standard of the hotel and anyone who has stayed in the Coco Chanel Suite at the Hôtel Ritz in Paris over the last few decades might have been forgiven for thinking a rather grand-looking Old

Master depicting 'The Sacrifice of Polyxena' was more than likely a 19th-century pastiche. However, during the recent renovations at the hotel a consultant by the name of Joseph Friedman noticed the letters 'C L B F', which, after a little more research, proved to be 'Charles Le Brun Fecit'. It was also dated 1647. Although the history of the picture was archivally unclear, it's thought that César Ritz may have acquired the picture in 1898 when he purchased the 18th-century building.

It was sold by Christie's in Paris for €1,441,500. Perhaps it's worth looking at the hotel art a little more carefully in future!

<hr />

Architectural Salvage

I've owned some interesting Beatles memorabilia over the years. Currently one such oddity is a brown manila envelope addressed to John Lennon at his childhood home, Mendips, 251 Menlove Avenue, Liverpool, now preserved by the National Trust. Strange to think that he probably opened it. I also own one of Ringo Starr's suits, which I occasionally wear.

It seems that anything associated with the Beatles is

collectable and I've been lucky enough to handle all sorts of objects on the *Antiques Roadshow*. If I had to pick a favourite it would most likely be a jacket that once belonged to John Lennon. I tried it on and as I put my hand in the pocket I discovered there was some rolling tobacco still languishing there.

One Beatles-related lot that recently caught my eye was a front door offered by Dominic Winter Auctions. It wouldn't have likely been given room in a salvage yard as the eight-pane glazed 1950s design is particularly undesirable for modern tastes. However, this one came from Paul McCartney's childhood home at 20 Forthlin Road, Allerton, Liverpool, where he lived from 1955 to 1964. It wasn't in good condition and had been salvaged from a 1970s refit at the house and purchased at a charity auction by the vendor. The National Trust – also custodians of that house – restored the dwelling to the same mid-50s style, installing a perfect replica of the door! Imagine that over 100 famous songs were written behind that door and it's not hard to see the attraction for Beatles fanatics. It realised £4,100.

Quack Cure

Almanacs were extremely popular publications in 19th-century America. As with most periodicals, the publishers sold advertising space to supplement their income, and given the vast volumes that were retailed, this would obviously have been an effective way of getting messages across to potential markets. As a result, manufacturers, particularly those of patent medicines, realised that they could advertise very successfully by issuing their own almanacs. Consequently, a new style of free almanac became prevalent, printed with eye-catching colourful covers extolling the virtues and efficacy of their remedies. Naturally, they

A typical American patent medicine almanac from the year 1885

used all manner of typical ploys such as beautiful women and healthy young children. It's estimated that by the late 19th century a patent medicine almanac was printed for every two Americans alive.

It was during this period that the number of European immigrants entering America soared, with millions passing through the notorious gates at Ellis Island, New York. Of course, they spoke a number of different languages and some companies were obviously astute enough to target all manner of different groups. Ayer's published their almanacs in 21 European languages!

An Ayer's Dutch-language almanac published in America in 1890

Auction Sniper

The snipe is a genus of wading bird that roughly incorporates around 25 different species. It is notoriously difficult for hunters to shoot as it has a very erratic and unpredictable flight pattern. Apparently, the word 'sniper' became popular in the 18th century as a mark of the skill required to shoot them, and as such became a term that we associate with military sharpshooters.

However, the connotations of the word are also difficult because the job of a sniper is obviously to 'take out' soldiers on the battlefield; and, far worse, they often have associations with wreaking havoc among civilian populations caught up in conflict zones. Hardly surprising then that auctioneer Moore Allen & Innocent found themselves in a little bit of a spot when they inadvertently reported the hearsay history of an item in one of their sales.

Formerly in the collection of an eccentric collector, the sale comprised a number of unusual lots, ranging from taxidermy to a photograph of the atomic bomb exploding at Christmas Island, some with rather apocryphal tales attached to them. It seems that Group Captain Samuel Rexford-Welch may have had a bit of a passion for elaborating a little on the past history of some of his possessions. One of the items was a skull, which he maintained was that of a Japanese sniper who had shot him in the leg and killed his driver while in Burma during the Second World War. Apparently Welch had then instructed a group of Gurkhas to 'take him out' and his skull had subsequently been kept as a trophy – gruesome, to say the least. However, when the story was reported, protests from the Japanese Embassy and other individuals led to an immediate withdrawal of the said skull.

Had the complainants read the description they would have realised that the skull was in fact thought to be a Victorian anatomical specimen, with the auctioneers merely attaching Welch's fanciful tale as an apocryphal footnote. Like many skeletons retailed in the 19th century for anatomical purposes, most originated from the East, particularly India. Given that there was absolutely no intention to upset anyone, the auctioneers undertook a professional evaluation to properly substantiate the age and origin of the skull and it was indeed proved to be 19th century and of Eastern origin.

It's a symptom of the business that many collectors are rather interesting characters with fertile imaginations – it comes with the territory. That's why auctioneers are often a little bit sceptical of provenances unless there is some tangible evidence to support such claims.

Apollo Apostles

'Space flown' or 'moon-landed' items have a great deal of cachet among collectors of space-related material. Wristwatches worn or owned by astronauts that have circled the earth are treated like national treasures and can make fortunes if they come up for sale. The whereabouts of each watch is meticulously recorded (although some are missing) and include Omega Speedmasters (standard-issue astronauts' watches supplied by NASA) worn by space legends such as Neil Armstrong. Ron Evans' Rolex worn on the Apollo 17 mission sold for $131,459 in 2010. Even a toolkit from the Apollo 17 mission sold for a staggering $75,900, such is the appeal of space memorabilia! However, the story of the microfilm lunar Bibles is a fascinating insight into the risk and sheer courage of the many people who worked on the Apollo space missions, particularly the astronauts.

Following the terrible launch pad accident in 1967 in which all of the crew of Apollo 1 – 'Gus' Grissom, Edward H. White II and Roger B. Chaffee – were killed in the command capsule, which was burnt out during a launch rehearsal, the Reverend John Stout formed the Apollo Prayer League. This was set up to pray for subsequent Apollo missions and to further the idea mooted by Edward White that he would like to take a copy of the Bible to the moon.

Given the weight and space limits on board the craft, microfilm technology was used to produce a copy of the King James Bible, and the Reverend eventually gained permission to have this included on the Apollo 12 mission (the sixth manned flight). Unfortunately, it was stowed in the command module rather than the lunar module and didn't make it on to the moon. A second attempt on Apollo 13 was also unsuccessful when the inclusion of 512 microfilm copies narrowly survived a catastrophe when an oxygen tank exploded and the crew – James A. Lovell, John L. 'Jack' Swigert and Fred W. Haise made their epic trip back to earth in a largely crippled craft, immortalised in the film *Apollo 13* with Tom Hanks. (Incidentally, the toothbrush from the mission owned by 'Jack' Swigert, the character played by Kevin Bacon, recently sold for $11,794.)

Third time lucky, the Prayer League were able to send 300 copies on the Apollo 14 mission, making sure that 200 were in the command module and 100 in the lunar module (allowing for all eventualities). 100 were finally taken to the moon on 5 February 1971.

One set flown on all three missions was recently offered for sale by RR Auction of Amherst, New Hampshire in the USA. Bound in a gilt-tooled leather folding cover with certification and a jewelled presentation frame, it sold for a very commemorative $130,000. It's known that many have been cut over the years and presented to dignitaries. It's thought that around twelve complete copies remain.

Poisoned Chalice

Mary Ann Cotton (born Mary Ann Robson in 1832) was one of the 19th century's most notorious serial killers. During her 40 years she murderously worked her way through around 21 victims, including her mother, three husbands and fifteen of her own children and stepchildren. Like many before her, she used arsenic to dispatch her targets, a method largely undetectable given the then level of forensic expertise and the prevalence of gastric-related diseases that so commonly took life in the period. A horrible, painful death, by all accounts.

Constant moving and taking several different husbands also made her crimes less detectable but she was eventually apprehended due to the fact that a suspicious local parish official called Thomas Riley was concerned at the death of her only remaining son, Charles Edward. She seemed more intent on collecting the insurance than anything else (she had collected on quite a few insurance policies). Tests for arsenic on samples taken from Charles proved positive and

Mary was sent for trial and subsequently hanged at Durham gaol on 24 March 1873. No one knows the true number of her victims but her notoriety was such that even the hangman apparently shortened the rope to make her suffer more.

So it generated some interest when a Bible appeared in a lot at Tennants Auctioneer's in Leyburn, bearing the inscription 'Bought of Mrs Cotton, William Lowrey' and thought to have been with her in Durham gaol before she was executed. The lot also contained eight letters written to a Lowrey who had looked after her affairs while she was in prison. The rather macabre lot made £2,200.

Mouse Man

I can clearly remember my mother handing me Franz Kafka's *The Metamorphosis*. I was about fifteen years old and quickly worked my way through the novella, transfixed by the inexplicable and totally mysterious transformation of Gregor Samsa.

Kafka's seminal existentialist work is often described as one of the most important pieces of 20th-century fiction and a mirror to his troubled, anxiety-ridden personal life centred around feelings of dread and uselessness.

Despite the important archival material already held by the Bodleian Library and the *Deutsches Literaturarchiv* (German Literary Archive) in Marbach, the two institutions also made a momentous joint purchase of 'Ottla's letters' in 2011, a collection from Kafka's youngest sister comprising 100 'autographs' (letters and postcards) and 32 other letters from Kafka's last lover Dora Diamant and his doctor Robert Klopstock. The price of the collection was undisclosed but it was an unprecedented collaborative venture that will further cultural access and use of Kafka's writings.

As an illustration of the potential value of such work, the documented sales trail of items is always interesting and the famous 'mouse letter', a four-page handwritten letter sent to Max Brod, the author, journalist and biographer of Kafka in 1917, has an interesting track record. It was written from his sister Ottla's Bohemian farm where he was trying to recover from tuberculosis. The letter is mainly about his fear of mice, which seem to have infested the farm. The missive has passed through several private collections over the decades, usually coming up for sale at the specialist saleroom of Stargardt in Berlin. It was first sold in 1981 and reappeared in 1997, selling for £12,700. The importance of the letter to scholars has always invited lively debate, with many arguing that it should be held in a public collection to allow access, rather than its infrequent sale through the hands of wealthy 'autograph' hunters. The £39,670 it achieved in 2011 when it was again sold to a private collector was too much for either the Bodleian or German Literary Archive to pay. However, its more recent emergence finally took it out of the marketplace for good with the intervention of several private benefactors who purchased it for £77,420 and donated it to the archive in Marbach. Never again will it have to suffer the bustle of the saleroom.

Fakes and Fortune

No year in the art world would be complete without its share of fake and forgery stories. One of the biggest centres around a Chinese painter called Pei-Shen Qian, a resident of Greenwich Village in New York and a jobbing artist who made just about enough money to pay his rent by doing quickly executed portraits of passers-by. Sounding familiar? I'm not sure what it is, but the idea of artists scraping a living and then turning to forgery as a way of cocking a snook at the art establishment always seems like a latter-day Robin Hood-type exploit worthy of some jovial wrist-slapping 'don't do it again' repartee. However, Qian's art was soon to take on another dimension after a chance meeting with Jose Bergantiños Diaz.

Diaz, along with his brother Jesú Ángel and his former girlfriend Glafira Rosales, masterminded a scheme that is estimated to have netted around $80 million from artworks forged by Qian. The artist himself strongly denies that he was forging works, but was merely copying the styles of famous painters such as Mark Rothko, Willem de Kooning and Jackson Pollock. Apparently, Diaz asked Qian to produce works similar to such luminaries and paid him between $5,000 and $9,000 a canvas. The canvases would then be aged with tea, left outdoors to acquire patina and doctored with hair dryers to age the paint. Added to this were the fake provenances concocted by Ángel and Rosales.

Apparently, the ruse became highly profitable when the venerable New York art dealers Knoedler & Company became involved in 'unsuspectingly' selling examples of Qian's work as works by great artists such as Rothko. The gallery, in business since 1846, had been retailing the works for the best part of two decades – after due diligence – and the art establishment was totally shocked when it suddenly closed its doors in 2011 amid accusations of selling fakes. Collectors and investors had paid millions of dollars for the forged works sold by the gallery; Qian, the seventy-five-year-old artist quickly slipped back to China, probably never to have to face the music back in the USA.

It's here that my admiration for Qian stops. Faking pictures is not really art. Anyone who has a modicum of talent can copy or emulate a living artist, particularly the abstract expressionists. Nothing of the original artist's thinking, evolution or skill can be conveyed in a straight copy or stylistic pastiche. This is merely a story about greed and avarice.

I thought I'd try my own hand at knocking off my own 'Rothko'. Here's the result. It took fifteen minutes ... perhaps Rothko on a bad day?

Golden Shower

I lived in the south-west of France for almost eight years. I bought a large house, steeped in history, complete with priest holes, 19th-century wagons and traps in the barn and most members of the original family conveniently located in the village graveyard a couple of kilometres down the road. Like everywhere I've lived, I've always wanted to know everything about the house, its inhabitants and the history of the surrounding area. What I've often found, if it didn't already exist, was a local latent curiosity, often simmering under the surface but waiting for a chance to boil over. So, usually when I've arrived somewhere, I prepare a light supper for the interested parties, snoop around their cabinets of historical ingredients and then turn up the gas to cook up some good results. Having made friends with my neighbours, mostly farmers, I was fascinated to find that they were more than happy for me to root through their boxes of family photographs. The result was truly amazing. The village was able to collate an exhibition of many hitherto unseen photographs of its inhabitants and architecture dating back well over a century, although mutterings about the new *rosbif* taking a rather forward approach to local history were of course always going to be par for the course.

However, the project led to many a good evening around the dinner table talking about the location of old Roman villas plundered by my guests when schoolboys and hoards of coins stashed in the walls of local barns. Coins were a regular theme of conversation and the local builder, spurred on by my enthusiasm, proceeded to buy a metal detector and arrive almost daily, using me as an erstwhile local finds liaison officer and museum identification service. On one occasion he unearthed a Charles I silver shilling just down the lane from my house, which he kindly presented to me as a memento. I've always been a little baffled as to how an English 17th-century coin was dropped in such a remote area of south-west France, but who am I to reason why?

Favourite among the tangible local treasures were the collection of over 100 19th-century gold twenty franc pieces that had been concealed in the wall of my friend's farmhouse – around £20,000 at current prices – he was saving them for a rainy day. So it was with some interest that I read about a collection of gold coins to be sold at Bonhams in Los Angeles that compounded my view of Frenchmen choosing to stash their gains in the barn rather than deposit it in the bank, no doubt historically linked to a cash-based farming economy where the taxman came relatively low down on the list! By all accounts, a worker at the Champagne Lanson Bonnet vineyard near the village of Les Riceys had been working in a former grape-drying building when he disturbed some gold coins which apparently rained down on him. A more thorough search led to the discovery of no fewer than 497 American $20 gold coins minted between 1851 and 1928, untouched for almost a century and in generally very fine condition. It's thought that they were probably secreted by a wine producer who had traded with the United States and Britain in the 1930s.

The haul realised $945,000 including commission, with 100 per cent of the coins sold. The finder, described as a 'modest employee' of the firm, did rather well out of the discovery for under French law half of the value went to him. I suspect he cracked a few bottles of champagne to celebrate!

Poetic Stuff

Some years ago I rented the apartment on the Spanish steps above the Keats-Shelley House museum on the Piazza di Spagna in Rome. There, the museum dedicated to the most famous English romantic poets preserves the bedroom and final dwelling place of John Keats (1795–1821) perhaps one of the finest and most revered of all our poets. He died of tuberculosis aged only 25. Every day that I opened the front door I thought about how he had passed through it, perhaps even touched the very same door handle; every day, I filled my bottle from Brunelleschi's fountain knowing that Keats too would have drunk its sparkling waters … it was emotive stuff!

Keats' poems were not critically acclaimed in his own short lifetime but his reputation grew after his death. He

The Spanish Steps, Piazza di Spagna, Rome

had been writing poetry for about six years. It's thought that he only sold around 200 copies of the three volumes published while he was alive but his work is now regarded as some of the most important English poetical work ever published; his letters too remain the focus of a highly regarded body of literary thought, providing a window on the philosophy and consciousness of a young man who ultimately was unable to fulfil his potential, having died so young.

Very few poetry items related to Keats ever come to the open market. Three draft parts to the poem 'I stood tiptoe upon a little hill' written in his own hand are recorded. Two were sold in 1929 and came from the collection of the American bibliophile A. Edward Newton. They have not

been seen since. Just one other piece, a copy of the son-
net 'To Hope', was sold in 2001 by Christie's for £88,400.
So it was amid great anticipation at the sale of the Roy
Davids Collection held by Bonhams that the third known
and much-revised draft of 'I stood tiptoe upon a little hill'
came up for sale recently. Despite being only one-thirteenth
of the text, the manuscript, written on both sides of a piece
of paper, was sold for an all-inclusive £188,250. Bonhams
claimed in their catalogue description that it is likely to
be the only poetical Keats manuscript to made available to
collectors. That's unless the other two ever come to light.

Moon River

Childhood memories of the *Andy Williams Christmas Show*
play a comforting part in my nostalgic view of growing up.
Roll-neck jumpers, scarves and marshmallows toasted on a
studio campfire seem integral to those 'comfort' reminis-
cences. Williams, who died in 2012, was an American idol,
a beloved crooner born in 1927 and raised at the height
of the Great Depression. His early days in a choir with
his three brothers led to a break as the backing singers on
Bing Crosby's 1944 hit 'Swinging on a Star'. Fame followed

and by 1947 they were playing in Las Vegas where apparently they were one of the highest-paid cabaret acts in the world. As a solo artist, Andy's signature tune was 'Moon River', Henry Mancini's 1962 song from the film *Breakfast at Tiffany's*.

What, you are perhaps wondering, does all of this have to do with the world of art and antiques? Quite simply, Andy Williams was a connoisseur collector of impeccable taste and amassed an amazing, eclectic art collection that encompassed everything from Impressionist and Modern art, to Oceanic art, folk art and decorative arts. Here's Andy:

Throughout my life, I have always been collecting. Every picture I ever sold I still regret. But I never gave up buying ... I could not imagine a life without paintings. I look at my paintings every day. At night I will go into the living room and look at the Dubuffet because I love it so much. Then to the drawing room, to look at the Picasso, the de Kooning, the Diebenkorn. I could not imagine a room without art ...

My first interest was French impressionist painting but of course I didn't have any money. So, I bought prints, $2 or $5 a print. I was about 25 years old. I was early in my career ... When I made a little bit of money, then I started to buy lithographs for $75. That's how I could afford Picasso. But that is all I could afford. When I started to make money I started to buy pictures. But that was in the 60s.

After his death the dispersal of the bulk of Williams' collection was conducted by Christie's and took place in New York, London and Paris over a six-month period and in ten separate events. Additional sales, including his collection of Navajo blankets, were handled by the likes of Sotheby's; this one was a sale of only 61 lots which raised just short of $1 million!

It was however his art collection that caused the biggest stir. The appearance of works by many of the world's greatest post-war and contemporary artists, which Williams displayed in his Moon River Theatre and at his California and Missouri homes, fostered great interest. Willem de Kooning's 'Untitled XVII' realised $9.7 million and Jean-Michel Basquiat's 'Furious Man' realised $5.7 million. Williams' art collection was reported to have raised around $46 million. Williams will be forever remembered as a nostalgic footnote in many people's lives but for many others he will also be remembered as a great art lover and collector.

Traveller's Friend

The name Louis Vuitton is synonymous with the idea of luxury and high-end fashion. It is one of the most globally lucrative and recognised brands of the modern world with its distinctive interlocked 'LV' monogram adorning products ranging from handbags to jewellery, perfume and clothing. Forbes quoted the company's worth at $28.4 billion in 2013.

The business was founded in 1854 by Louis Vuitton. Vuitton had apparently observed the designs of other manufacturers and within a few years of opening the company was ardently promoting flat-topped stackable trunks, rather than the popular arch-topped trunks which helped with water run-off. His grey canvas 'Trianon' trunk quickly gained in popularity and, just like today, imitators were quick to catch on. To counteract these imitators, Vuitton implemented new canvas designs with a red and beige striped canvas in 1872 and a beige and brown stripe in 1876.

The company's first shop in London was opened on Oxford Street in 1885 and soon after, in 1888, the Damier canvas pattern was introduced with the inception of the trademark 'LV' signature logo. Vuitton died in 1892 and the management of the company passed to his son George who continued to push the company on the world stage by exhibiting at trade fairs such as the Chicago World's Fair in 1893.

The patented symbols proved successful in reducing counterfeiting and the business expanded across the globe with the Vuitton signature store opening on the Champs-Elysées in Paris in 1913. It was the largest travel goods store in the world. Despite a well-documented and profitable collaboration with the Nazis and Philippe Pétain's puppet government during the Second World War, the company eventually progressed out of family hands to become the unassailable global brand that it is today.

I have on a few occasions filmed antique Vuitton trunks on the *Antiques Roadshow*. They are extremely popular and have always been a favourite among interior designers, who like to use them as set dressing and centre tables. I remember staying in Anouška Hempel's Hotel, Blakes, around 20 years ago and balancing my glass on the edge of such a trunk, surrounded by black hessian, tiger-stripe fabrics and Piranesi engravings – all very much of the time but rather luxurious!

Values have continued to rise for all areas of the luxury vintage luggage market and none more so than Louis Vuitton products. Shabby late 19th and early 20th-century trunks continually realise several thousand pounds at auction. An exceptional example at Christie's, covered in the 1876 striped canvas, recently confounded the estimate of

£4,000–6,000 by rocketing to £30,000. It's thought that this is a world record for a Louis Vuitton trunk, surpassing the previous high of £20,000 for one sold in the USA in 2012.

By George

I love miniature objects and I recently purchased a 10cm-long copper alloy cannon. It bears the inscription 'Royal George sunk 1782' and is one of those emotive little objects that harbours an incredibly emotional story.

HMS *Royal George* was a 100-gun ship of the line, launched in 1756. At the time, she was the largest warship in the world and saw service in numerous major battles and engagements, serving under a number of distinguished commanders as the flagship of several admirals. Her notable endeavours included action during the Seven Years War and at the battle of Quiberon Bay in 1759. After extensive repairs between 1765 and 1768 she returned to service with the Channel Fleet and was again refitted at Portsmouth in 1778–79 before seeing action against the Spanish and aiding in the capture of 21 out of 22 Spanish merchant and naval ships while en route to relieve Gibraltar, an engagement which under the command of Admiral Sir George Rodney was urgently needed to help supply the garrison there. The ships, from the Spanish Caracas Company, were escorted back to England as bounty. This success was followed a few days later by the defeat of a Spanish fleet at the Battle of Cape St Vincent and the subsequent relief of Gibraltar on 19 January 1780.

On returning to England, her hull was coppered, a practice which protected the wood and cut down drag, enabling ships to sail faster. In 1782 she was anchored off Portsmouth effecting various repairs with a full complement of crew on board, readying to relieve Gibraltar yet again. As well as the crew, there were around 200–300 extra visitors, including women, children and a number of merchants who were trading items with the crew. The repairs included shifting the guns to the central line in order to 'heel' the ship over for work on the hull; unfortunately, a misjudgement sent her past her centre of gravity and despite an order to pull the guns back, it was too late. A lighter (barge) was tied alongside loading provisions, some of which were being passed through the lower gun ports and she started to take in water and rapidly keeled over, her masts bearing down on the lighter, slightly delaying her imminent demise.

Countless people were trapped inside. Admiral Richard Kempenfelt perished in his cabin, trapped by the pressure of the water, and around 800 other crew and visitors drowned in the disaster. The captain, Martin Waghorn, survived. It was England's worst maritime tragedy. Many of the victims were washed ashore at Ryde on the Isle of Wight. They were buried in a mass grave, now the site of Ryde Esplanade.

An enquiry and court martial never attributed specific blame to any individuals. Instead, the disaster was attributed to rotten timber that gave way under the stress of the heel.

The poet William Cowper penned this sad verse:

> Toll for the brave
> The Brave that are no more,
> All sunk beneath the wave,
> Fast by their native shore
> ('The Loss of the Royal George', 1782)

Salvage of the wreck proved difficult for the technology of the day. The ship had sunk in a busy channel and the masts were protruding above the waterline. Fifteen guns were initially raised by Charles Spalding, the Scottish amateur engineer and diving bell designer. It wasn't until 1834 that further work was carried out by diving engineers the Deane brothers and more guns were recovered. In 1839 Major-General Charles Pasley of the Royal Engineers used diving equipment to raise another 30 guns over a three-year period. He also recovered many personal items and raised countless timbers, including the keel. The site was finally declared clear after a massive controlled explosion using lead-covered barrels of gunpowder. The explosion apparently broke windows as far away as Gosport.

And here is where my little copper alloy cannon can finally tell its story. The great billiard table in Burghley House was made of wood salvaged from the ship. George Wombwell, the famous menagerie owner, was interred in his tomb in Highgate cemetery in a coffin fashioned from the wood of the *Royal George*. Some of the bronze cannon were melted down to cast the base on Nelson's column, and other small objects such as my cannon, were also created as small souvenirs of the great tragedy. From the 18th-century naval glory of the world's largest gunship to the seabed of the Solent to my study – priceless!

Machine Age

I remember from boyhood the numerous antiquated-looking chromium-cased vending machines and weighing scales that dotted Britain's high streets, bus terminals and station concourses. I also remember trying to fool them with foreign coins – a threat now largely combated by electronic coin detection systems! These days, they are glitzy refrigerated glass-fronted larders rowed up in 'full-line vending' ranks, less prone to the frustrated hammering of a cigarette-less clenched fist than the smash and grab of a hungry ram-raider. Perhaps it's nostalgia but collectors love old vending machines. Retro-decorated kitchens and warehouse apartments still suit the surreal appeal of a machine that's made for a public place being supplanted into the domestic environment.

Among the rarest survivors are the huge cast-iron machines from the Victorian and Edwardian period which were mostly scrapped as they became outdated or required for the war effort (for their scrap metal). They include some spectacular examples supplied by the Sweetmeat Automatic Delivery Company, established in Britain in 1887 as the first vending machine installation and servicing company. 'Sweetmeat' is a very old-fashioned word used to denote confectionery or food items. In the 18th century it was in common use to describe delicacies such as crystallised fruits and sugared almonds. The firm closed in 1904 and machines displaying its trademarks rarely come to the market.

One machine that did recently come to auction was a handsomely restored 'column and drawer' example with no fewer than eight vertical dispensers for products such as 'Chocolate Cream', matches and throat pastilles. Refinished in red with white coach lines, it made £7,500 against an estimate of £800–1,200.

❧❧❧

Fork and Knife

I like to set a good-looking table for dinner guests. The cutlery drawer in the sideboard represents around 250 years of flatware history, with a selection of utensils ranging from agate-handled Georgian beauties to the more durable 19th-century King's pattern plate that graces the table at Christmas time. I remember quite vividly how, around twenty years ago, my early ideas about keeping things period meant that I would only use original Georgian steel-bladed knives. This required me to invest in a 19th-century rotary knife polisher to keep the easily marked and rust-susceptible knives serviceable. No matter how debauched an evening had taken place, it was never possible to leave them overnight – the damage would be just too great. I stopped short of banishing electric light and modern conveniences from the house but after a few years and with no staff, I did invest in some stainless steel-bladed knives to ease the effort of catering along historic lines. (In more recent years I had obviously forgotten the rigours of culinary historic re-enactment as I battled with syllabubs from 19th-century recipes that wouldn't set. I think I've now learnt my lesson.)

Certain areas of flatware collecting motivate a curious connoisseurial type of interest; spoons are one such area. The use of forks at the meal table only became popular in the 18th century. Prior to this, the spoon was the common general-purpose eating utensil. For those that could afford a silver example, the surviving seam of sometimes rare assayed specimens fuels a market for collectors intent on accumulating certain regional variations; trefid spoons (a type with a pair of notches in the terminal to split it into three sections), engraved and decorated, often personalised with initials and sometimes dated, are a favourite. Perhaps one of the most outstanding and well-documented examples is the Romsey-Ashburnham gold trefid spoon made in the reign of Charles II by Robert King and assayed for 1681. The spoon had originally belonged to John Romsey, a Colonel in Cromwell's army and co-conspirator in a plot to kill Charles II. Its rarity and history brought a healthy £31,750 in the Christie's sale of 2001.

A notable collection that came to sale in 2007–08 was that of the Canadian collector Mr Britton Smith, an avid collector of early spoons. The situation was complicated by the implications of an amazing case centring around the silver forger Peter Ashley-Russell, which took place at

Snaresbrook Crown Court in September 2008. Here, it transpired that Ashley-Russell had been producing extremely good fake early trefid spoons and selling them into the market. In all, around 39 objects were used in evidence against him, including some clever conversions from spoons to forks, which as I touched on earlier, are far rarer, and are hence far more valuable. A report by The Goldsmiths Company makes fascinating reading and is illustrated with photographs emphasising the extraordinary lengths that he went to in forging extremely convincing fake punches with which to mark pieces. Despite the potential to derail consumer confidence at the Britton Smith sale, some outstanding examples did rather well, including a Henry VIII 'lion séjant' spoon (boasting a terminal in the form of an upright lion) which made £13,500 and a diamond point spoon of the same period which made £10,500.

In 2010, Lyon and Turnbull of Edinburgh offered a very rare Puritan spoon reputedly found in the gardens of Barncleuch House. Scottish silver always carries a premium among the niche collectors and this example was marked for George Cleghorne and assay master Deacon Andrew Burrell for 1653–55, bearing the initials 'QH/MD', most likely for Quintin Hamilton and his wife Marion Denham of Barncleuch House. It made £27,000.

More recently, and bringing us up to date, was the emergence of a very rare pair of Irish trefid spoons, another niche area for silver collectors. The pair, thought to be only the second known extant, carried a Dublin mark of 1676 for the maker Edward Swann and were initialled 'SSM'. Cheffins of Cambridge's 'come get me' estimate of £800–1,200 was soon surpassed and they went on to realise £25,000 – perhaps the highest price ever paid for Irish flatware?

Muck and Brass

Earlier on in the year I was commissioned to write a series of articles on Wiltshire towns and villages. I decided to tackle Devizes first, a historic town with lovely architecture and a traditional brewing industry manifested in the slightly austere, red-brick Victorian cathedral-like temple to brewing of Wadworth. I had a wonderful guided tour by the manager, sampled the product – naturally – rooted through the 19th-century recipe books and was astounded by the continuation of traditional skills still supported by the company, such as the work of the sign-writing shop and the wonderful shire horses that continue to make the deliveries in town. I've never seen so much Brasso in my life!

So, do you know what a hame plate is? You'll certainly have heard of horse brasses; hame plates form a subdivision of the same category of collectables and are one of the decorative elements that make up traditional horse harnesses. Hames are long, curved metal or wooden (or a mixture of both) arms that encircle the neck of a horse. They are an essential part of the harness used to pull drays or carts and you'll have seen them on the lovely shires that traditionally pull brewery carts and on parade horses. The hames are bridged by a section of leather and this is mounted with a brass hame plate. These come with all manner of decorative schemes, sometimes multiple plates or roundels, often emblazoned with patriotic mottos such as 'God Save the Queen' (or King).

People often think of horse brasses as a vernacular, clichéd type of object, wholly unfashionable in this day and age and a vestige of old-fashioned public house decoration and cottage fireside ornamentation. To be honest, I have yawned on a few occasions but mainly because – on the whole – they don't sell very well at auction. However, there is a National Horse Brass Society and the history of the brasses, which goes back to the middle of the 19th century, is quite compelling. It's generally agreed that the earliest examples are cast but by the 1880s they were being stamped out in profusion as part of a larger industry. There are over 2,000 different designs recorded but with the demise of the heavy horse their popularity accordingly waned.

My favourite brasses are actually the fly or head terrets which adorned the top of the horse's heads, often known as 'swingers'. I've frequently amazed visitors to the *Antiques Roadshow* by explaining what they are. Out of context and mounted on wooden bases, people have largely lost track of their original use. The best collection available to the public is that of the late Dr Kirk of Pickering in Yorkshire, housed in the Castle Museum in York.

Among the most collectable brasses are those issued for 'best in show' by organisations such as the Royal Society for the Prevention of Cruelty to Animals (RSPCA). They fervently promoted the idea of parades, the London Cart Horse Parade being the most famous, to instil a sense of pride and compassion among the owners of working horses and to improve conditions for the thousands of horses on the streets of Britain. It's interesting to note that the collecting of such brasses was already popular in the late 19th century and an article in a 1916 edition of *The Connoisseur* magazine highlights the appearance of fakes – nothing's new!

Thimbleby & Shorland, the Reading auctioneers, hold specialist sales of carriages, harnesses and related material. One sale not long ago demonstrated this interest with the appearance of a brass for the Dunmow Horse and Cart Parade 1907. It was awarded as a first prize to an E. Richardson and made a hefty £800.

Ugly as Sin

Many years ago, when I was cutting my teeth as a young auctioneer, I visited a rather gruff and aged lady whose personal circumstances were a little precarious. She had little in the way of financial resources and was in jeopardy of being put into a home. Her dog, which she adored, was a major problem because she was finding it difficult to look after and naturally couldn't bear the idea of being separated from her beloved pet. She directed me to root through the cupboards to try and find something that would help solve her problems. As I opened various old pine dresser doors and rummaged around, it all felt a little hopeless until one door revealed an object that proved to be rather special – a true eureka moment. There, staring at me from a shelf, was a Martin Brothers 'Wally' bird, a grotesque pottery 'jar', the body and head modelled as a crow-like creature with a wonderful 'following' eye. I took him in for sale and for several weeks he sat on my desk and stared at me, finally realising a very healthy £9,000! This enabled the lady to stay in her home and pay for extra help. She wrote me a lovely thank-you letter – less gruff than on our first encounter.

Robert Wallace Martin (1843–1923) was the eldest of four brothers. He and siblings Charles, Walter and Edwin worked together with complementary roles to run the now famous Martin Brothers pottery. As their eccentric identity

The Martin brothers

became established, their output evolved to encompass a whole range of salt-glazed 'art pottery' items ranging from vases and plaques to 'spoon holders' and 'grotesques'. Their innovative style and challenging production put the brothers at the forefront of studio pottery design; subsequently they have come to be known as the 'founders of the modern studio'. Much of the pottery was characterised by flora and fauna, borrowing from the Japanese aesthetic, but Robert, as the chief 'thrower', made the amazing creatures that have come to epitomise the Martin Brothers studio. The Wally birds (after Wallace) are the most sought after, and values continue to rise. A large characterful example recently sold by Woolley and Wallis auctioneers was snapped up by an American buyer at a world-record price of £81,750. Not bad for an ugly old bird.

Odd Societies

I am frequently asked by interesting groups and societies to lecture and talk on all manner of subjects related to art, antiques and history. This, I'm glad to say, is a strong indicator that the homogenisation of society is safely being held at bay by a die-hard phalanx of dedicated people who preserve, protect and promote some of the strangest aspects of our cultural heritage through the formation of odd societies. I don't use the word odd in a derogatory fashion, merely to indicate that some of these organisations are concerned with some quite offbeat aspects of antiques and history.

In these days of the internet there are those that don't have to rely on a formal organisation, just a website and various interested parties contributing to an online archival record of aspects of our disappearing heritage. The Ghostsigns project is one such venture; participants have been collecting photographs and information on remaining hand-painted wall signs all around the UK. These are mainly 19th and early 20th century and are fast fading – hence the name.

Among my favourite groups is the Pylon Appreciation Society. Few would think an electricity pylon worth considering but for some they are beautiful! I'm also fairly keen on the idea of preserving historic corrugated iron buildings such as meeting halls and chapels. Corrugated iron has been around since the 1820s and it helped to build the British Empire; it formed distinct styles of architecture in the early settlement of countries such as Australia and New Zealand. Plenty of people appreciate its history!

Some further examples of interesting societies are listed in an appendix on page 301.

Gothic Sleeper

Dreweatts Auctioneers were obviously a little bit dubious about the construction and origins of an oak plank chest that was offered in their salerooms as part of the residual collection of Laurence William Hodson, brewery owner and connoisseur. I'm prone to moaning about the sheer quantity of coffers and plank chests that I've seen over the years, mainly because people don't really want them. Lots of lovely 'mule' chests and trunks dating from the 18th and 19th centuries have no perceived place in modern households, mainly because they are quite impractical. They make good television stands but then you can't open them to access the storage space. I usually encounter them stuffed full of vintage Christmas decorations, a fact that denotes that they are often only opened once a year!

Over the centuries and particularly in the 19th century, many such coffers and plank chests were reinvented by latter-day upcyclers. Front panels were cut and hinged to make small cupboards; elements were used in other pieces of furniture, particularly the carved front panels; otherwise plain chests were embellished with additional carving and spurious dates, which no doubt made them a little more desirable.

The Dreweatts plank chest was, however, a little different. According to the catalogue it was described as 'probably constructed from 16th/17th-century elements with later restorations and repairs' – a euphemism for 'we're not putting our necks on the line'. The estimate was £800–1,200. However, the style of decoration and construction certainly looked considerably older, featuring geometric, arcaded, foliate and spiral roundels and Gothic details. The metalwork also looked period. Conjecture was rife but the general consensus was that the chest was probably 15th century and of French or Anglo-French construction. It sold for £20,000!

Game Off!

Racial stereotypes and racism are as old as history itself. That's not to excuse it: racism is abhorrent and its banishment should be paramount in the modern world. However, the historical vestiges of its legacy are manifested in many different ways and I have come across many examples. One area where racism prevailed was in children's games, an obvious example of the perpetuation of stereotypes by play – and we all know how powerful a tool learning by play can be!

Despite the racial and derogatory overtones of such

games, there is a strong demand for original examples, particularly in America where Black Americana is heavily collected by some prominent black Americans. It's a market where counterfeiters also operate. Not all items have negative connotations and objects collected might range from advertising material to postcards. However, many people believe that's it's important that we continue to emphasise the historical trials of oppressed people by keeping this material available so that we never forget. There are those that might condemn even this article but I too believe that it is important to look at such items in their historical context – not to say that I'm not shocked and flabbergasted by some of the items I have come across during my career. 'Five Little Nigger Boys' dating from the 1950s is one such game, comprising a cardboard box in the form of a wall with five stereotyped figures and an elastic band gun to shoot them off!

A much earlier game came up for sale at Brightwells of Leominster. It was part of a collection of antique games collected by a local schoolteacher. Entitled 'The New and Fashionable Game of the Jew', boardgamegeek.com lists it as published in 1807 by Dunnet & Wallis (John Wallis Snr). Featuring a stereotypical rendition of a Jewish banker in the centre of the board, the game apparently revolves around making or losing money. It's quite a rarity and is keenly sought by collectors. This was a rather shabby example but still realised £720.

Promise to Pay

Who invented the first banknote? To be frank, I'm sure most people would guess correctly. It was of course the Chinese. Bills or promissory notes originated around 2,000 years ago and were made of leather. They became popular in the Tang (7th century) and Song (11th century) dynasties among merchants, as a form of lightweight substitute for carrying out transactions, particularly where heavy coinage might be involved. In this form they were a type of receipt or a piece of paper that guaranteed payment, perhaps within a limited period. These were as good as money and when the central government realised the benefits of printing portable paper money it passed a decree to gain a monopoly over the printing of such currency. Initially, it was geographically limited and set with a time limit for use but during the years 1265–74 this changed and a nationwide variant was printed, state-backed by precious metal, making it effectively a guaranteed form of payment. In other words, it could be trusted by the general population as a valid and redeemable form of payment accepted everywhere. This was an idea that even in Europe persisted until the advent of the First World War with the gold standard.

Explorers and travellers in China such as Marco Polo noted the paper money with great interest and effectively introduced the idea to Europe. In his book *The Travels of Marco Polo*, he outlines in one chapter 'How the Great Kaan Causeth the Bark of Trees, Made Into Something Like Paper, to Pass for Money All Over His Country'. As the founder of the Yuan Dynasty, Kublai Khan used paper money to fuel the state and Westerners like Polo were impressed by the power of these seemingly worthless pieces of paper backed by the power and wealth of the state.

From the beginning of the 12th century, the Chinese were utilising intricate designs, special woven papers and coloured inks to foil the forgers and by the 14th century Europeans had firmly grasped the idea of the promissory note, later to become what we know as a banknote. The tradition of banknotes backed by gold is still historically incorporated into our British notes with the words 'I promise to pay the bearer on demand the sum of [for example] £5'. With the demise of the gold standard the note can now only be exchanged for other notes but there was a time when it could have been exchanged for gold.

A Ming dynasty banknote issued by the Emperor Hong Wu (1368–1398) was recently sold in Hong Kong. The note was block printed on Mulberry paper, a resilient and durable medium which lasted well in circulation. This one had obviously lasted particularly well and it realised £7,140.

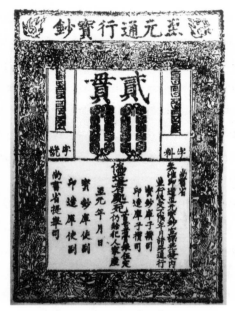

A Yuan dynasty banknote

Our Pictures

In 2003 the Public Catalogue Foundation launched a massive project to photograph and list all of the oil paintings held in public ownership throughout the UK. Understandably, this was no mean feat and not only involved the galleries and museums but also paintings in public buildings such as town halls, universities, hospitals and fire stations. The idea was to make them available, along with relevant information, on the BBC's Your Paintings website, a project launched in 2011.

Eighty per cent of the pictures generally are not on view to the public and many had never been photographed, other than perhaps for an insurance valuation at the local council offices! The whole project is a charitable endeavour supported by various luminaries from the art and auction world and its endeavour to feature as many works as possible has led to around 215,000 pictures by around 37,000 artists being made available to view online, with details about location and history. The recent culmination of this work was an upload of some 40,000 works. The most prolific artists listed are John Everett (1,058 works) and Marianne North (1,034 works). I've found it enormously helpful in researching material; nothing can quite prepare you for the sheer diversity and wealth of art that is held in the public collections of this country – just take a look, at www.bbc. co.uk/arts/yourpaintings.

Chelsea Boot

Black leather: it's a classic rebel look. Film stars and pop stars alike have always sported leather jackets and none more symbolic than James Dean and Marlon Brando in their Schott Perfectos®. In 1954 Marlon Brando appeared in

The Wild Ones, stoking a rebellion that reverberated through the American system, a mood symbolised by a jacket that was subsequently banned from schools for its association with delinquency. James Dean wore a Perfecto® too and his jacket can be seen in the Fairmount Historical Museum.

The rebellious black leather look also crossed the Atlantic and many European bands were heavily influenced by the style. In their pre-Ringo Hamburg days, the Beatles were completely leather-clad and rather rough-edged, a look that Brian Epstein steered them away from, eventually putting them in collarless suits and black Chelsea boots.

Typically, the appearance at Bonhams of over a dozen Beatles-related lots, sent to auction directly by George Harrison's family, created a great deal of interest. One of the objects was a black leather jacket worn by George in Hamburg. Purchased during the Beatles' residency between 1960 and 1961 and also worn at The Cavern Club, it had passed directly through the family, even being worn to school by George's nephew in the 1970s. The iconic jacket can also be seen in the famous publicity shots that feature Pete Best and Stuart Sutcliffe. Considered by many to be one of the best items of Beatles clothing to come on the market in recent years, it sold for a commission-inclusive £110,450. A custom-made pair of George's black Chelsea boots –particularly rare survivors dating from 1964 – sold for an inclusive £61,250!

Head Hunted

I've collected some pretty macabre objects over the years and although it would be wrong to call it a treasured possession I do own one artefact that would make most people's hair stand on end. It's a cannibal's cassowary bone dagger from Papua New Guinea. Of course, cannibalism is one of the greatest taboos. Throughout history we have been captivated and intrigued by tales of cannibalism, whether performed by indigenous populations of far-flung tropical islands, such as the Maori massacre of the *Boyd*, a convict ship which in 1809 lost most of the 66 people aboard, or the story of the *Essex*, a ship sunk by a sperm whale in the Pacific in 1820 with the two sole survivors reportedly found in a boat, gnawing on the bones of their shipmates. It's a subject that is both repulsive and strangely compelling, and artefacts associated with cannibalism occasionally come up for sale.

An example of such an object is a Fijian cannibal fork. Usually carved from wood and comprising four long, sharp prongs, they were used by priests and chiefs who ritualistically didn't touch their food. So although they were used to eat all foodstuffs it's highly conceivable that any antique examples would have also been used in the consumption of their vanquished enemies. The problem with many tribal artefacts is the dating. Such forks are still made for tourists and finding antique examples with good provenance and good patination is hard. A selection of seven entered by a private collector at Martel Maides Auctioneers on Guernsey were deemed period – probably mid-19th century – and attracted international interest. They sailed by their collective £1,600 bottom estimate to make a tasty £25,600.

⸎⸎⸎⸎⸎

Tall Story

The artist and collector Jean Willy Mestach died in March 2014. His collection of African art was considered by many to be one of the best privately assembled selections of the genre, all hand-picked by a man who understood both the aesthetic and spiritual symbolism of the material he gathered around him.

One of the most published objects and a piece frequently seen in photographs of Willy in his studio, was the 2.5m tall Nkundu reliquary figure from the Democratic Republic of Congo which he acquired from a gallery in Brussels after the Second World War. It was sold by Christie's in Paris, a city now recognised as a centre for the sale of tribal art, for a staggering €2.35 million.

Bulldog Blues

Fighting the tide of fakes and forgeries is a constant battle in the antiques and art business. To be frank, most of the objects I encounter are not even good enough to be called fakes; rather, they are just poorly executed pastiches of the real thing – not to say that this doesn't fool the layman. Part of the fascination with divining the plethora of rubbish allowed to pass loosely catalogued through the sales of many unconcerned auctioneers and trade establishments is the sheer cheek of the (mostly Far Eastern) fakers.

This last year, the main trends seem to have been Austrian 19th-century-style cold-painted bronzes; the usual surfeit of 'ox bone' Chinese erotically decorated boxes and snuff bottles; some cleverly embellished Regency tole (painted metal) trays with rather lovely looking clipper ships (which incidentally are the wrong period for this type of tray); Victorian table-top octagonal wooden postal boxes; cast-iron and alloy signs supposedly dating from the 19th century up to the 1950s; brass scientific instruments, mainly compasses and telescopes, which have been flooding the market for several years; novelty cast-iron door stops and umbrella stands; countless designs of Vesta cases (matchboxes); a glut of skull-related items made to cash in on the popularity of memento mori, such as cane handles and tobacco boxes; 'jades'; Nazi items, made in incredibly poor taste, ranging from dress daggers to table-top 'officers' snuff boxes; cufflinks made of 'silver' decorated with foxes' masks and hunting scenes; and desk clips in Victorian and Edwardian styles, again often made in the form of foxes' heads.

The usual suspects still abound and have almost become part of the fakery woodwork: signs, novelty cocktail shakers, netsukes, tin toys, tea caddies, etc., some of which have been reproduced for so long they almost feel like antiques. Interestingly, it's part of the way the world works and when I'm long dead and gone I suppose it's quite likely that some of these things will be catalogued in sales as 'Victorian Revivalist', a mere 100 years old rather than the 200 they are meant to be!

A recent story in the trade press recently caught my attention, for although I have yet to actually come across one, I was amazed to see how a fake French papier-mâché growling bulldog had gone through an auction, only to be returned by the purchaser as a 'clever and recent reproduction'. The object of the article was obviously to highlight that these were infiltrating the market. Having sold at £750 and a collectable that sometimes realises in excess of £1,000, these are the sort of low-key but relatively good value items that make faking worthwhile for the perpetrators. One begrudgingly has to occasionally marvel at their skill ... albeit momentarily.

Of course, I pride myself on not being caught out but I was recently taken in by something that played quite cleverly on my male predilection for a nice leg. The things in question were at an auction sale and comprised twelve 19th-century *cartes de visite* of a titillating nature. Each card (and they really were 19th-century) sported a sepia photographic image of a lady, generally in stockings. The backing cards were definitely period and embossed in gilt with the name of the photographic studio, all French – as these cards are most likely to be! They were contained in plastic wallets and due to the size of the view and being subject to the usual time-management issues, I didn't remove an example, although I was happy that they looked fine. On purchasing the cards and returning home I carefully examined them out of the wallets and noticed that although two photographs had the same photographer's cipher within the print they were on differently named studio cards. A quick slice with a scalpel and all was revealed – these were very good aged-up Fuji prints stuck on 19th-century cards, complete with the original photographs of rather more adequately dressed ordinary folk lurking underneath. Lesson learnt but money returned by apologetic auction house who asked what they should do with the others that were designated for forthcoming sales. You can imagine what I said. The moral, I suppose, is one that I often preach to people: if it looks too good ... need I finish?

The honey trap!

Poles Apart

Vice Admiral Sir George Strong Nares (1831–1915) was born in Abergavenny. His highly distinguished naval career took him on all manner of expeditions and he was renowned as a leader and explorer. He was the first man to command a ship through the Suez Canal and mounted several famous voyages including the search for Rear-Admiral Sir John Franklin and his crew who went missing on their quest to chart the North West Passage in the ships HMS *Erebus* and HMS *Terror*. The ill-fated expedition was last seen in Lancaster Sound on 26 July 1845 by the crew of a whaler. Despite numerous attempts to locate them, a few graves, some minor traces and notes remained the only clues to their demise. Although the expedition had set sail with three years' worth of provisions, the canned food had been secured at the last moment from a cheaper source and is now thought to have been soldered with poorly constructed lead seams, which were thought to have given the crew lead poisoning, adding to their sad destiny.

An expedition in 1850 found some minor evidence of the men. Inuit testimony says that the crew eventually abandoned their icebound ships and tried to leave on foot. The witnesses also attested to the crew resorting to cannibalism and this was reported to the Admiralty in 1854 by Dr John Rae, who was conducting a surveying expedition.

The horrific news was leaked to the British press and caused disgust among the Victorian public. Rae's career was ruined by Franklin's widow, who strove to keep her husband's reputation intact. Countless searches were mounted over the years with no conclusive results. In fact, more people died searching for the expedition than were originally lost.

In 1984 three crewmen buried on Beechey Island – they had died early on – were exhumed and autopsied. Up until 1992, other discoveries, including a quantity of bones from some of the crew, found on King William Island, were also used to provide samples for testing. High lead levels were identified, lending weight to the tin can theory, although they were so elevated that it's also now thought that the ship's water system could have contributed. Analysis also revealed blade marks on the bones, strongly indicating that in the pitiful final throes of trying to survive, the crew had cannibalised their fellow mates.

Back to Nares. The search for Franklin gave him valuable exploratory experience and was an important factor in gaining him command of HMS *Challenger*, a steam-assisted pearl-class corvette launched in 1858 and famous for the oceanographic Challenger expedition of 1872–76. Knowledge of the oceans was at that point rather scant and extended little further than a few fathoms. The purpose of the expedition was to find out more about the depths of the seas and the *Challenger* was well equipped with laboratories and equipment, plus eighteen miles of rope for deep-sea dredging and sounding. A special platform was installed for the dredging and thousands of jars and large quantities of material for preservation were taken aboard. The voyage covered an estimated 70,000 miles with in excess of 4,000 new species catalogued or preserved.

In 1875 another Arctic expedition was launched and Nares again took charge of the search for the North Pole. The two ships on the British Arctic Expedition were *Discovery* and *Alert*. Nares became the first captain to take a ship through the channel between Greenland and Ellesmere Island. It is named in his honour – as are several other places! The expedition was a dangerous undertaking and the crews were badly struck with scurvy as well as a lack of suitable clothing and equipment. Nares retreated before the ships could be locked into another winter of ice but a record was set by a sledging party who made it the farthest north of any expedition to that date.

I once filmed a rather lovely freedom casket on the *Antiques Roadshow*. Such caskets are presented to those granted the freedom of towns and cities and the recipients usually include local dignitaries, elder statesmen and philanthropists. The caskets are often finely constructed from silver with enamelled panels, although I have also seen some well-executed wooden examples. They contain a vellum scroll which grants the freedom of the said municipality, also finely executed in the best calligrapher's hand. It was therefore with some interest that I spotted an exceptional casket in an impending Woolley & Wallis sale, in the form of a loaded sledge and dated 1876. The extraordinary design of the casket by Hartmann and Bauscher of London was very unusual: the sledge itself was balanced on carved mother-of-pearl simulated ice and snow. It had been presented to Vice Admiral Sir George Nares by the Worshipful Company of Shipwrights and bore the arms of the City of London, Nare's personal crest and the Arctic Medal. The unthoughtfully low estimate of £1,000–1,500 was quickly surpassed and it sold for a more rounded £11,000 – an historical object presented to a remarkable man and one I would have been keen to own.

POSTSCRIPT: Since I wrote this piece and just days before the Almanac is off to the printers the Canadian Prime Minister Stephen Harper announced that Parks Canada (the Canadian cultural and heritage agency) and the Canadian Hydrographic Survey had discovered one of the Franklin Expedition ships. The underwater images do not give enough clues as to whether it is HMS *Erebus* or HMS *Terror* but this amazing news will no doubt make another interesting story for the next instalment of *Allum's Antiques Almanac*.

Label Freak

As the markets have changed over the years and the demand for certain types of antiques has declined, some objects have become remarkably good value. The state of the 'brown' furniture sector continues to fuel saleroom gossip and even the man on the street seems to be a 'have a go' expert on the ins and outs of the antiques world: whether things will or won't pick up! Of course, the quality of 'brown' furniture (an expression used to describe standard types of domestic antique furniture) varies widely and there are plenty of quality, highly attractive pieces that are still worth owning, whatever the style pundits are preaching! 'Incorporating it into the modern environment' is my mantra and I continuously chant it in my mission to re-popularise the idea of well-made antique furniture married into the demands of modern living.

I inhabit a very old house, some parts are 15th century, but that doesn't mean that I'm wedded to comparative date-related artefacts and period furniture. I like to mix it and you'll find post-war art on my walls happily sitting next to 17th-century portraits. To be frank, I like a bit of theatre and it's the affordable theatrical that makes it so much fun buying at auction.

Dining rooms are always pleasurable rooms to accessorise. Large early 19th-century mahogany sideboards and buffets with integral lead-lined cellarets and chunky gadrooning always provide the main focus for a wealth of potential decorating opportunities. I love glass; heavily cut Georgian pieces glint beautifully in candlelight (one of the reasons for cutting them as such) and decanters look majestically formal and proper arranged on old Sheffield plate trays and decanter stands. Victorian decanters are remarkably cheap at auction and a few facet-cut beauties are unlikely to cost you more than £30–40 each in a typical Saturday general sale. Finish them off with some decanter labels and your guests will usually enter into the prevailing dinner party spirit that builds around a well-set table. Sometimes known as bottle tickets, such labels were used to denote contents on a whole range of decanters and receptacles and could include sauces and beverages such as 'soy' and 'cyder'. Wine and decanter labels – as they came to be known by the late 18th century – come in a variety of shapes and sizes and usually take the form of a plate that is hung around the decanter neck on a chain. Silver and plate examples are the most common, but they were also made in enamelled metal, mother-of-pearl, ivory, ceramic and even silver-mounted plaques on warthog tusks. They range in date from the Rococo period to the modern-day and vary in style from rather plain rectangular plaques with clipped corners to oval 'navettes', reticulated (pierced) engraved and die-stamped specimens, to extremely fancy cast varieties heavily redolent of their intended use and decorated with vine leaves and grapes. They are very collectable and also quite idiosyncratic because the reasons for some being valuable are not always that obvious. Factors can include all manner of combinations including the name on the label, the makers, the material and the design. Even a spelling mistake can add to the interest.

Historically, some of the drinks that they denote have fallen out of common usage. Shrub is an interesting one; this was a very popular beverage in the 18th century. Based on brandy or rum with the juice of citrus rinds and added sugar, it was drunk either on its own or sometimes used as a base for punches. It had largely fallen out of favour by the late 19th century. Hollands is another interesting one, being a Dutch or Belgian gin, an old style distinctly different from the gins you and I know and based upon malt wine spirits. It was also known as 'jenever' or 'genever' and hence you sometime come across decanter labels with the word 'Geneva' on them, being the anglicised version. Many labels carry names such as 'Teneriffe', 'Madeira', 'Moselle', 'Lisbon' and 'Manzanilla', which denote regions or places of origin for a wide variety of wines, spirits and fortified wines.

Another one of interest is 'Bucellas'. The modern spelling is 'Bucelas' and it is a region of Portugal with the highest wine classification in the country (DOC). The wine was popularised in Britain by the Duke of Wellington, who discovered its merits during the Peninsular war and sent large quantities back to his home. It became very fashionable in London and hence the labels were made. I particularly liked a die-stamped example misspelt 'Bucellos', made in 1820 by Edward Thomason – an unusual variation and worth around £300 on the open market.

Examples by Scottish silversmiths are always sought after and Woolley & Wallis recently offered a good collection of 68 such labels, of which an example engraved with 'Hollands', very plain looking but by the silversmith William Innes of Tain (fl. 1830–1870), made £3,000. Another, inscribed 'Madeira', realised £2,500. Of course there are cheaper examples around and if you fancy a plain old rectangular Victorian 'Claret', it will cost you less than £100.

Stolen Goods

Objects often harbour secret histories, stories locked within them, usually never to be known but sometimes revealed by the clever investigations of resourceful researchers or inquisitive auctioneers. This was the case with auctioneer Philip Rance of Netherhampton Salerooms, who when confronted with a rather fine Mughal silver spice box in the form of an Indo-Persian Khula Khud (helmet), noticed a compartment within the box. He prised it open in front of the vendor to reveal a note upon which an inscription stated that the box had been looted during the siege of Delhi in 1857 by Captain – later Major General – Ellis Cunliffe of the First European Bengal Fusiliers and that it was probably from the palace of the last Mughal Emperor, Bahadur Shah Zafar II. The box had been handed down through the family, all the while harbouring its well-stashed provenance. Like many objects looted through our imperial past, it held a great attraction for potential buyers and surpassed its £2,000–3,000 estimate to make a spicy £10,500.

Owls of Shame

I can't think of a more majestic, captivating, not to mention allegorically and mythologically connected creature than the owl. A rather fabulous barn owl lived – of all places – in my barn, and my mother has a pet Indian Eagle owl called Genghis. He's beautiful. So why would you want to shoot one? To be frank, most people wouldn't, and besides, all wild birds are now protected. However, in the 19th century it wasn't quite the same situation and this was highlighted by the most unusual lot that came up for sale at Sworders Auctioneers of Mountfitchet.

An album embossed with gilded lettering reading 'The Wynyard Park Owl and H.R.H. The Prince of Wales, Oct. 23rd, 1896' told the extraordinary tale of a visit by the Prince to the house there. It contained various photographs and correspondence related to the royal guests – and a picture of a stuffed owl, which, apparently, having been shot by the Prince, was subsequently stuffed on the instruction of photographer John Phillips and mounted with a plaque stating that the Prince had shot it. Phillips then sent a copy of the photograph to His Royal Highness! Apparently, the Prince was not at all amused and this resulted in a 'grovelling' apology from the photographer to the Prince. A very quirky story but one that boosted the album, estimated at £400–600, to a much stronger £2,700!

Credit Crunch

We take them completely for granted – small standardised rectangles of plastic embossed with our names and encoded with information that allows us to pay for goods just by hovering them near a terminal. However, credit and debit cards are just one of the myriad applications that magnetic strip technology affords us (security cards and travel tickets are among the other things that we similarly take for granted). It's a development that in the last 50 years has completely revolutionised our lives.

Credit cards are not a new invention. Individual companies have applied the idea of credit, guaranteed by the issue of a card, for almost 100 years, but the idea of a universal card that could be used at more than one place was not seriously addressed until the 1950s. The idea of a centrally controlled system began to take shape in the 1960s with IBM's development of magnetic strip technology. Magnetic tape had already been in use for decades and the idea of using it to store data had also been in practice since the Second World War. IBM's development of fixing magnetic strips to cards had begun in the late 1960s at their Information Records Division. Fixing the strips to the cards proved problematic; the solution was apparently inspired by the wife of Forrest Parry (who along with Jerome Svigals was the leading engineer on the project). She suggested ironing the strips on. This method of heat-bonding the strips worked and so the magnetic swipe card was born.

Two prototypes were initially produced and featured magnetic cellophane tape glued to a card base. One is kept in the Computer History Museum in California; the other, until recently, was still in Jerome Svigals' wallet! It was sold by Sotheby's New York for $19,000.

Touched by the Devil

It seems archaic that anyone would be ostracised for being left-handed but throughout history and perhaps even in some cultures today, being left-handed was commonly associated with being evil, threatening, malicious or in league with the Devil. Historically, the word 'sinister' has its root in the Latin *sinistra* meaning 'left' and although we often regard left-handed or ambidextrous people as being extraordinary or perhaps talented, they were historically treated with great prejudice.

There are of course many famous left-handed people but I've always been fascinated by left-handed guitarists. I'm a right-handed guitarist; I can't play the other way around. However, Jimi Hendrix could play a guitar either way up simply by turning it over, without even re-stringing it. This meant that he could play the guitar upside down or the right way around – a rather incredible skill. Apparently, his natural inclination was to be left-handed but his father

Al, by all accounts, pressed him to play right-handed due to that age-old belief about the Devil! Initially, Hendrix did restring his guitar but his ability to just flip the instrument over, putting the treble E at the top, was an amazing idiosyncrasy of his playing. Like me, Hendrix couldn't read music, which made his approach to playing rather esoteric and abstract – not that I'm trying to compare myself with him! In fact, nothing was really conventional about the way Hendrix set his guitars up. He used custom string sets and because his guitars were flipped, which put the controls at the top rather than at the bottom, this caused tonal differences associated with the body cavity of the instruments; and there was also the fact that the bass string then had a longer reach to the machine head. Complicated?

Well, it certainly didn't mean that Hendrix was allied to the Devil but it did mean that he developed one of the most original playing styles and sounds in the history of rock music. Of course, Hendrix is also famed for burning his guitars on stage, the first of which he torched at the Finsbury Park Astoria in 1967. It was sold at the Fame Bureau's Rock 'n' Roll auction in 2008 for £280,000. Most recently, the Fame Bureau also offered Jimi's black Fender Stratocaster which he played in 1967 at the Monterey Pop Festival. It was the first US appearance of his group, The Jimi Hendrix Experience. The guitar was sold for £180,000 – strung upside down, naturally.

Sporting Life

It's always a joy to be handed a museum-quality object, the type of thing that you often only get to see through the glass of a museum cabinet. A high point of the last *Antiques Roadshow* series was the arrival of a late 16th-century crossbow, which I was tremendously excited about. My favourite place for looking at such objects is the Wallace Collection in London, but suddenly, out in the wilds of Wales at Gregynog Hall I found myself handling such an item. It transpired that it had been purchased in the 1960s from a 'junk' shop in Tunbridge Wells for £3 – quite a lot of money considering the man was actually an impoverished student at the time, but still a bargain nevertheless.

The history of the crossbow is fascinating. I remember many years ago visiting the great Terracotta Army of the Emperor Qin Shi Huang (the first emperor of a unified China) near Xian and being attracted to a bronze mass-produced crossbow trigger, an object emblematic of the army in some respects, being a 'factory-made' part that enabled less skilled but highly effective swathes of men to use a powerful 'point and shoot' weapon with great effect. The Chinese had even invented a repeating crossbow!

Traditional bowmen have always been held in great esteem, mainly because the art of archery is a great skill generally honed over a long period. Not so with the cross-bow, although its more cumbersome design and slower rate of fire were obvious negatives compared to a longbow, for instance. However, just about every culture in every epoch has used some variation on the mechanical catapult or its close cousin the crossbow and so we see it manifested in both large siege forms and the more portable forms such as the one I filmed on the *Antiques Roadshow*.

Ancient Greek crossbows known as *gastraphetes* and Roman versions are well documented and bear a remarkable similarity to the later medieval crossbows. Large siege versions, sometimes mounted on stands and called *Wallarmbrust*, were often used in siege and castle defence situations. Another well-known name for a crossbow is the French *arbalest*.

Given the increased power of a crossbow, loading and tensioning such a weapon could be quite difficult and was done in several ways. Foot stirrups (the metal loop on the nose) were used to hold the bow steady on the floor while it was drawn; a pull-lever or push-lever comprising a long arm to pull the string back was another alternative; or there was a windlass, which comprised two rotating arms either side of the butt, or a rack-and-pinion *cranequin* (also known as a 'cric' or 'rack') which, again, mechanically drew the string back with a rotating arm. French cavalry who were armed with crossbows were known as *cranequiniers*.

Naturally, such crossbows were particularly lethal and armour could easily be penetrated by some of the gruesome types of bolt that had been designed for just that purpose. With the advent of firearms, the goalposts were moved yet again, although the crossbow still remained popular. French First World War soldiers used them for launching hand grenades over the top of trenches and crossbows are still used in some modern military applications although their fearsome reputation makes them unpopular among critics in civilian life and hunting scenarios.

The wooden crossbow I filmed at Gregynog was ornately inlaid in horn, most likely stag horn with delicate trailing scenes of foliage and forest creatures – hares, bears and deer – and of course this artistic narrative is what gives the game away. Crossbows were excellent for accurately and silently pursuing quarry in the forest. A similar hunting

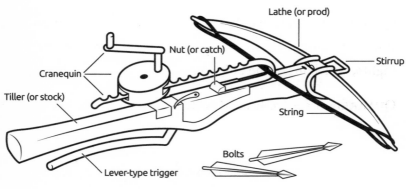

A 16th-century crossbow

crossbow sold with Hermann Historica in Munich for £21,740 although the one I saw on the *Roadshow* was missing a few parts and worth less at £2,000–3,000. Good value for a 400-year-old item!

Crossbow bolts do not have fletchings (feathered flights) and vary in design from incendiary versions to barbed hunting examples, although there are some limits to the design given that the bolt has to travel along a channel. A few different types of bolt are listed below. The crossbow was a favourite of the Italians (the Genoese in particular were renowned for their prowess in war), hence the profusion of Italian names!

VERRETTO: A long Italian bolt of 25 inches with an iron conical point, used for target practice.

PULZONE: A large bolt with a blunt tip, most commonly used to stun the target.

QUADRELLO: An Italian bolt with a gruesome reputation; it has a pyramidal tip with a square base and leather folding flights, which make the bolt spin.

QUARREL: A square-headed bolt.

Sole Survivor

No one can deny the poignancy of the centenary commemorations surrounding the anniversary of the beginning of the First World War. For that reason 2014 has become a year of unparalleled interest in the stories and artefacts that surround the history of 'the war to end all wars'. This phrase is slightly ambiguous, as its patriotic and idealistic origins (when the conflict was first described as 'the war to end war') gave way to a more cynical degree of scepticism based on the ever increasingly huge and pointless loss of life. However, that does not distract from the overall feeling for those who gave their lives in the Great War and few symbols can be more poignant than that of the poppy, an enduring reminder of the tenacity of a flower that populated the battlefields and graveyards to become the universal symbol of remembrance in 1921.

I don't suppose it would have occurred to many of us that such a flower from the battlefield might have survived or be of any commercial value. However, a poppy thought to be the only surviving example, picked from a trench in 1916, recently came up for sale at Duke's of Dorchester. It was picked by Private Cecil Roughton in a trench near Arras. He was only seventeen years old. It was pressed along with its leaves and mounted in an autograph book. Roughton gave it to a Miss Joan Banton in 1923, inscribing it in ink with the words 'Souvenir from a front line trench near Arras, May 1916'.

Before coming up for sale, the poppy had been exhibited at a special exhibition staged by the British Legion. It is now encased in an acrylic block. Estimated at £500–1,000, it sold for £6,344 (including buyer's premium). It was purchased by Hancocks, the jewellers who hold the royal warrant to make the Victoria Cross, Britain's highest military award for bravery and valour.

Serious Burns

I'm not a full Scot but I like to lay claim to my Scottish ancestry on my mother's side so that I can don my Grant hunting tartan, dust down my sporran and celebrate Burns night with whisky, haggis and readings of the work of Robert Burns, Scotland's national poet. The Scots have an unswerving admiration for Burns and, among other titles, know him as simply 'The Bard'.

His works include a tranche of romantic poems, songs and lyrics including 'Auld Lang Syne', *Tam O' Shanter*, and 'To a Mouse'. Burns' iconic status and literary legacy elevated him to a cult-like personality in his romantically tumultuous and relatively short life (he died aged 37). He fathered twelve children, only nine of whom were by his wife Jean Armour, yet he maintained, despite his promiscuity, that she was always his true love. As a result, Burns has several hundred living descendants scattered around the world!

So, invested with a bit of Scots blood and a passion for celebrating the man on 25 January, I'm always interested to see what Burns-related objects make when they come up for sale. I'm even more enthused when I come across something myself, as I recently did on an interesting probate valuation.

Among the contents of an old strongroom was a leather case embossed in gilt with the words 'Burns' Bottle'. The key, which was tied to the top, wouldn't reach the lock, so I fiddled for few minutes to undo the old twine and eventually opened the box. Inside was an 18th-century decanter, lacking the stopper (and, incidentally, fitting the case perfectly without it, suggesting the stopper had been missing for long time), engraved with Masonic devices and mounted with a silver collar. Engraved on the collar was the inscription 'This bottle belonged to the poet Burns and presented by his widow to Miss Catherine Reid 1834'. These are the sort of moments that make my job worthwhile.

This decanter forms an interesting link to Burns' Freemasonry associations, which have perhaps been lost in time somewhat to most Burns aficionados and historians.

Few people realise that he was a Mason and that he was the Senior Warden of Lodge St Andrew in Dumfries when he passed away. Of course, I can't discuss the whereabouts of the decanter; that's the family's business. However, just having held it is enough to fire the Scot in me!

A good yardstick for its potential value would be an object such as the 18th-century pocket watch which came up for sale at Lyon & Turnbull Auctioneers of Edinburgh. The back of the case was engraved 'RobT Burns Mauchline 1786', the provenance reinforced by the inclusion of a paper insert in the case decorated with hearts and initialled by his wife Jean Armour, 'the belle of Mauchline'. Interest was intense and the draw of Burns was attested to by the fact that it made £32,000.

Best Offer

Apparently, it's becoming a lot more common for dealers to call up auction houses and make an offer for something in the catalogue before it comes under the hammer. This is a dilemma for both the auctioneer and the vendor because, firstly, the auctioneer is obliged to tell the vendor of any offers; and secondly, some of the offers can be considerably more than the auctioneer's estimate. I'm not criticising auctioneers in general but the vendor's expectations are sometimes held in check by 'come get me' estimates and also the potential problems of a common-or-garden difference of opinion about how old an item actually is. There are also all sorts of other indeterminate factors that might influence a dealer to make a pre-emptive offer, such as the thirst for new, fresh-to-the-market stock, or an order that needs to be filled, pronto. Given the level of some offers, weighing up the pros and cons of accepting or letting the lot continue to auction is quite a difficult decision and despite the fact that it's mainly trade customers that do it, it's a practice that most dealers find highly annoying, particularly if they are prepared to travel and chase a lot that they really want, only to find that it has been sold before the auction.

Recent examples of this phenomenon have occurred at Sworders of Mountfitchet, where a George I gilt console table which was estimated at £3,000–5,000 was quickly withdrawn by the ecclesiastical vendor following an offer of £100,000! Latterly, a pair of Neoclassical mahogany pedestal cupboards described by the auctioneers as Adam-style and of late 19th century in date were estimated at £600–800 but caused a pre-sale offer of £20,000 plus expenses. Apparently, some dealers thought they were period and others thought that they were late 19th-century 'in the style of '. Although the pedestal cupboards were not technically a true pair (the doors opened in the same direction) their origins from a deceased estate led those responsible to let them proceed to public auction. This turned out to be a well-calculated gamble when the hammer went down at the considerably higher amount of £50,000!

In God We Trust

I own a metal detector. I've never used it much, although I've often found it useful when I've mislaid my tools while chopping wood in my woodland. Nothing worse than losing your 'twister' wood-splitter! The main purpose of buying it was to gradually search several acres of my property in France in the hope of finding some buried treasure. Optimistically thinking I would leave the best until last, the natural spring full of Roman votive offerings (a typical ritual place to deposit objects) tantalised me and while I found plenty of spent gun cartridges (the French are big on hunting), the odd coin and an 8th-century bronze brooch, alas, the spring yielded absolutely nothing of any value.

However, the situation was totally different for an American couple in California who in 2013 were out walking the dog on their land somewhere in the Sierra Nevada. Known as John and Mary, their true identities and the location of their incredible discovery have been kept confidential but the enormity of their find, known as the saddle ridge hoard, certainly hasn't. The couple had plied the route of their discovery on several occasions but on one particular day they noticed a rusty metal can protruding from the ground. The can was very heavy, and eventually split due to its fragile state, revealing gold coins inside. They returned to the site with tools and eventually used a trusty metal detector, which resulted in the recovery of eight cans holding a total of 1,427 gold coins in $20, $10 and $5 denominations. The coins were dated between 1847 and 1894 and constituted the largest buried hoard of gold coinage ever found in the USA.

The face value of the collection came in at $27,980 but the true value of the collection began to become apparent as the specialist company of Kagin's were brought in to provide a valuation. They in turn contacted the Professional Coin Grading Service (PCGS) to grade the collection, which revealed that some of the 'Double Eagles' (a rare and valuable type of US coin) were uncirculated and mint or as good as any other known examples. An 1866 $20 'no motto' Double Eagle was valued at around $1 million and estimates for the collection were thought to be around $10 million.

As is often the case with such discoveries, conjecture

was rife as to where they had come from and who had buried them. At one point it was thought that they might be the unrecovered spoil of a robbery committed in 1901 at the San Francisco Mint by an employee called Walter Dimmick, but this stumbling block was dismissed as the dates of the coins did not tie in. Various fortune hunters came out of the woodwork but none had a credible claim. In the end, the truth remains an enigma and I suspect we will never know who actually buried the coins.

In the meantime, some of the hoard has been sold on Amazon (under 'collectibles') and at the time of writing there is still quite a good selection available for sale. Perhaps your chance to own a little bit of American history – at a price!

Whipped Up

*The only traditions of the Royal Navy
are rum, sodomy and the lash.*
(MISATTRIBUTED TO WINSTON CHURCHILL)

The barbarity of naval discipline is legendary. Popular culture portrays the harsh regime of being at sea in the

18th and 19th centuries with press-ganged sailors being keelhauled and flogged for minor offences. Often used in films and novels, the angry and beleaguered crew are forced to watch as tyrannical (or sometimes justified) captains maintain discipline or push them ever closer to mutinous behaviour. This was the cruel and ruthless reality of serving at sea on both naval and merchant vessels.

Keelhauling was the practice of tying a sailor to a line which was looped under the ship and throwing him overboard to be dragged under the keel. This could result in serious injury and mutilation caused by the abrasive nature of barnacles and growths attached to the hull – or worse still, drowning. This practice was abandoned by the Royal Navy around 1720.

Flogging might seem like the lesser of two evils but the indicted crewman would be clamped in irons and given 24 hours to make his own cat-o'-nine-tails – the infamous whip used to flog the unfortunate sailors. Apparently, the boatswain would select the nine best knotted cords and they would be mounted on a wooden handle, traditionally red. Some accounts describe different variations including 'cats' with cords continually knotted or with knots on the ends. Some cats would have metal barbs added, which was a particularly sadistic addition to the amount of injury the whip could cause. The number of strokes was by all accounts limited to twelve lashes per offence but no doubt would be apportioned in a way that saw much heavier punishments meted out. This would seriously wound the offender, leaving his back raw – and it was then traditionally rubbed with salt (albeit more for its antiseptic properties than to increase his pain).

Several other punishments could also be used, including the notorious 'running the gauntlet', typically used for theft, in which the offender would initially be lashed with a continually knotted 'thieves' cat' and would then pass between two lines of the ship's company, who would lash him again with ropes, while opposed by two officers who kept him at sabre point to ensure that the pace was limited to a slow and painful walk. He would then be given a further twelve lashes. Gruesome! Flogging was finally abolished in the British armed forces in 1881, although its use had been generally discontinued sometime before that date.

So it was interesting to see that Charles Miller Ltd of London, specialist auctioneer of maritime-related artefacts, offered an example of an early 19th-century cat-o'-nine-tails, totally woven from rope, in one of his sales. He commented that he had never seen one come up for sale before, which may have been instrumental in the interest it garnered, finally selling to an American collector for £1,400.

Rude Letter

During the filming of a recent *Antiques Roadshow* at Belton House near Grantham I was lucky enough to come across the relative of a gentleman who had served for over twenty years as the Duke and Duchess of Windsor's chauffeur. I filmed a piece which included a silver Cartier cigarette case that the Duke and Duchess had presented to their loyal servant – it was a poignant and interesting tale of discretion and enduring faithfulness.

The story of King Edward VIII and Wallis Simpson is a romantic yet sad and much analysed tale of the power of love, politics and a constitutional crisis that led to the abdication of a monarch who served his nation for under a year. As a younger man, when Prince of Wales, he had a reputation for recklessness and his propensity for having affairs, particularly with married women, was a source of worry to the establishment. Freda Dudley Ward, socialite and textile heiress, was his mistress from 1918 to 1923; during that time they exchanged correspondence and would meet in secret to carry on their affair. Birmingham auctioneers Fellows were able to offer a very interesting letter relating to their romance, which was dated 12 May 1919. The rather explicit content refers to a secret rendezvous between the two at Freda's London apartment after a visit she was making to the opera. The Prince calls her 'My Darling beloved little Freddie' and is obviously besotted and very excited at the prospect of meeting her.

Such literal and personal missives are a strange insight into the private world of a part of society not typically publicised. Throughout history, we have tended to view such people as 'above all that' but typically they are always proven to be normal, full of the same human frailties that we all are – sometimes worse. This insight into Edward's life attracted serious attention from collectors of royal ephemera and the estimate of £1,200–1,500 was comfortably surpassed to make a final £5,100. Another part of the Duke's complicated and extraordinarily fractured life laid bare.

Fishy Tale

I've already touched on the tragic tale of the lost Franklin Expedition (*see* 'Poles Apart', *page 237*) but couldn't resist this associated tale of a gentleman by the name of George Edwards who was carpenter's mate on the steam yacht *Fox*. The *Fox* was a three-masted schooner-rigged auxiliary steamer launched in 1854 and purchased by Lady Franklin in 1857 to send out on yet another search for her missing husband and the crews of HMS *Erebus* and HMS *Terror*. The ship spent two years off the Boothia Peninsula looking for evidence of the men and it was on this voyage that the only written messages left by the crews were found, lodged in cairns on Prince William Island.

Geoffrey Breeze, one of the foremost dealers of antique canes, based in Bath, has a reputation for finding the unusual and rare and at a recent BADA (British Antique Dealers' Association) Antiques & Fine Art Fair he offered a walking stick with an amazing history. The cane, fashioned from a narwhal tooth (sometime referred to as a tusk but actually a giant incisor) had been brought back by the aforementioned George Edwards after the voyage. It's likely that as the ship's carpenter he personally made it, and the materials, probably traded with the local Inuit, included a walrus ivory screw-top that doubled as a snuff compartment. The cane was mounted on its return with a silver collar inscribed 'Brought Home In The Fox By Geo Edwards. Sent Out By Lady Franklin 1859'. The asking price for this perambulatory accessory? Somewhere around the £40,000 mark!

Ship Shape

Gebr. Märklin & Cie GmbH, otherwise known as simply Märklin, is a famous German toy company founded in 1859. It originally specialised in doll's house accessories but later expanded into other toys. The company name tends to be synonymous with model trains and its first system was produced in 1891, leading to the introduction of various different gauges including the large 0 gauge, the best examples of which are now highly sought after by collectors. This system includes the Swiss SBB Crocodile pantograph electric articulated locomotive, which comes in several different versions and can be worth thousands of pounds.

Märklin saw a profitable business in model trains because it enabled them to produce a whole range of associated accessories that would bring buyers back over a long period of time. This early form of 'upselling' included tinplate items such as stations and engine sheds. As a complement to their railways they also manufactured a number of other toys including motor vehicles, aircraft, submarines and ships, and it's the ships that often realise very high prices.

In 2012 a Märklin tinplate model of HMS *Terrible* from the collection of Ron McCrindell, the pioneer toy collector, made £76,000. Märklin's version of the protected cruiser takes some liberties with the design and has two funnels fewer than the original Victorian leviathan.

The real HMS *Terrible* (top) and Märklin's HMS *Terrible*

At the time, this was one of the highest prices ever paid for a single toy in the UK. However, the value of tinplate ships continues to climb and the market is particularly buoyant in the United States, where the sale of the Richard T. Claus collection has seen some perfect storms on the high seas of the auction scene. Two paddle steamers from his collection have been of particular note: the first, called 'Providence', sold in 2012 for $215,000. The second, larger steamer, dating from 1902 and named 'Chicago', was apparently contested by the underbidder who missed out on 'Providence' and realised an even heftier $230,000. The Claus collection of nautical toys made a massive $3.4 million in total.

Palace Bowl

The Ming Dynasty was one of China's greatest dynasties and oversaw an era spanning 276 years (1368–1644) of cultural, governmental and social stability and advance. Interestingly, when I was young, I always associated the word 'Ming' with objects of great value (and Flash Gordon's arch enemy), particularly blue and white porcelain; this association was and is widespread, and has become a bit of a cliché because popular culture fostered the notion that such rare and priceless pieces would always get smashed by some bumbling idiot in a comedy sketch. Hence, the Ming vase became the default 'fall guy' of any antiques or art-related joke and the most valuable object that could be broken by a clumsy camera-wielding tourist in a museum. This idea was ingrained in me during the 1970s but the current stratospheric rise in the value of Chinese porcelain and art has solidly reinforced this perception, although the highest values have not been achieved by Ming pieces.

However, it's still heartening to see recent results firmly asserting that Ming objects can still keep up with the like of some of the superlative pieces made for Qing emperors such as Yongzheng (1678–1735). Latterly, the most valuable was the Cunliffe musk mallow 'Palace' bowl sold in Hong Kong by Sotheby's (musk mallow is a biennial plant of the hibiscus or mallow family. Its seeds can be used for making perfume). The bowl, previously in the collection of one of the greatest collectors of Chinese art, Lord Cunliffe (1899–1963), is one of a class of Chinese ceramics of enormous rarity and quality, made in the Imperial kilns for the Ming Emperor Chenghua.

The kilns, at Jingdezhen, have been extensively excavated and the spoil heaps have provided amazing evidence for the volume and period of Imperial production. The production of the particular type of porcelain exemplified by the Cunliffe bowl was limited to a very short period, perhaps only ten years in the late 1470s and 80s, although opinion is divided. This particular bowl, prior to the sale, was one of only two left in private hands, with eleven others in museums – none actually in China, apart from reconstructed kiln site wares. As a result, this sensuous and distinctive ware made especially for the Emperor Chenghua is prized above most others for its fineness and subtlety of decoration, shape and glazes. It sold for $18 million!

Smallwork

It might seem rather inconsequential to most people but small novelty silver items, or 'smallwork' as the genre is known, are always attractive to collectors. As a result, I have to keep my eye open for objects that show a sense of clever innovation and originality. These often take the form of vinaigrettes, sewing implements, snuffboxes, vesta cases, card cases, nutmeg graters, propelling pencils, menu holders and so on. The different forms can be extremely varied and I've seen propelling pencils in the shape of harps, pistols, forks, barrels and pigs to name but a few.

This variety can be seen in all categories of smallwork and one of the foremost manufacturers of such objects was the London silversmith Sampson Mordan (1790–1843). He co-invented and patented the first mechanical pencil with John Isaac Hawkins – the innovation for which his company is probably best known. However, throughout its history the company – later under the ownership of Mordan's sons Sampson and Augustus – continued to make a whole range of interesting silver and gold objects until the factory was bombed out in the Second World War.

Vesta cases (from Vesta, the Roman goddess of the hearth and home) are widely collected and come in literally hundreds of different shapes. Made as matchboxes and initially used as a safe way of carrying rather unreliable early types of matches around, they became an essential fashion item of the Victorian period, along with snuffboxes and, of course, propelling pencils. Such items made statements about their owner's wealth and status and vesta cases came in humble plated base metals and pressed silver, right up to the high-quality enamelled examples executed by Mordan. That company's series of enamelled sentry boxes are highly collectable and many examples have been sold lately, some making well in excess of £2,000. The variety of designs is almost endless, with hunting scenes, railway tickets, dogs, coaching scenes, jockeys and flags to name but a few. A single-owner sale at Lawrences of Crewkerne in 2012 featured over a thousand examples by all manner of makers; more mundane examples were sold in multiple lots but the collection realised £75,000.

Another lot of smallwork caught my eye at Fieldings auctioneers of Birmingham, in the form of a group of three silver paint tins. Hallmarked for London and Birmingham at 1915 and 1916, they were an amazingly simple and almost surreal interpretation of an everyday object which would have been worthless had they not been reinvented in silver. They were the perfect present for an artist and the three made just over £500. Alas, there was no turpentine bottle to go with them.

Ivory Tower

The American version of the *Antiques Roadshow* recently banned the transmission of footage showing carved ivory tusks. Although it hadn't been showing overtly tusk-shaped items for several series, there had been increasing pressure and arguments from conservation and wildlife groups on the effect of screening ivory objects as a continual promotion of the trade. Many people think that this is a factor that con-tributes to the gunning down of literally tens of thousands of elephants a year. The Wildlife Conservation Society also issued a satirical video made in the style of an *Antiques Roadshow* appraisal, which was called 'Vintage Horrorshow'. It makes a strong point. Current legislation in the US has recently been changed and it's now illegal to trade ivory in the States unless it qualifies under strict CITES (the Convention on International Trade in Endangered Species of Wild Fauna and Flora) regulations. The screening of some objects, however, remains discretionary under such regulations and might include musical instruments that have an antique ivory content. And this is the problem. The new legislation in the US, at the time of writing, still allows 'sport-hunted' trophies to be imported – although personally I cannot see how this can be permitted in any way, shape or form. It seems somewhat hypocritical. However, the debate has widened enormously and we have also heavily deliberated the issues ourselves with regard to coverage of ivory objects on the British *Antiques Roadshow*.

Prince William's alleged recent comments about destroying all the ivories in the British Royal collection caused an absolute storm. Few from the world of art and antiques would have come out in defence of what he supposedly advocated: that is, the destruction of priceless antique works in ivory including such masterpieces as the throne presented to Queen Victoria by the Maharajah of Travancore, the throne on which she was photographed as the Empress of India in 1876. As a result, the press has been awash with stories about the future of the ivory trade and whether the Prince's comments were accurately reported or not. As a consequence, the wider debate has become very heated.

My colleague David Battie from the *Antiques Roadshow* wrote an open letter to the Prince in the *Antiques Trade Gazette* in which he commended the Prince's principled stance but likened such attitudes to those of despots and regimes who have destroyed the art and culture of previous societies and generations:

> Your highness, I have nothing but admiration for your principled stance, your obvious love of wildlife in general and of the elephant in particular, but I really don't think that destroying the one will preserve the other [...]
>
> Such iconoclasm has not been much admired by succeeding generations ... to witness a few: the Mongols, the Nazis, Khmer Rouge, the Roundheads, Mao Tse Tung and the Taliban.

What is obvious is that the trade in illegal ivory continues at an alarming pace and one of the main problems is the world's inability to stem the flood of modern carvings in antique style that hail from countries such as China. For a specialist in the antiques world it's not at all difficult to spot a modern ivory but for the average man on the street it is much more difficult.

None of us in the trade want to support this horrible slaughter but should we be held responsible for dealing in items with ivory escutcheons that were made 200 years ago? Does this support the killing of elephants? It's a difficult argument which has left us on the British *Antiques Roadshow* much of the opinion that we have to temper our approach to the subject. For that reason, if ivory is filmed, you will see contextual information and educational material used to balance the cultural significance of the object with the effect on black market demand.

Strangely enough, and in stark contrast to the issues surrounding ivory, interest in taxidermy has gone through somewhat of a renaissance. Again observing the legal restrictions of CITES, taxidermy has become a trendy decorating accessory and is particularly prevalent in the fashion and advertising worlds. So what makes selling an antique taxidermy tiger any different to selling an antique ivory carving? Well that's an argument I'll leave you to dwell on. However, tiger skins with taxidermy heads often come up for sale at auction, often with interesting stories attached. The legendary 'man-eater' that terrorised a village seems to be the most common story and that was the tale attached to a specimen offered by Moore Allen and Innocent of Cirencester. Shot in 1943 by a man called Henry Thomas

Jones, it was sold with an account of his expedition in the central provinces of India, together with a photograph of the dead tiger and the triumphant Jones. The tiger had apparently eaten the local schoolteacher's husband and no doubt this became the excuse for its termination. The lot sold for £1,900.

Interestingly, the taxidermy company that prepared that example have played a part in the history of the species. Van Ingen & Van Ingen were one of the largest and most famous taxidermists in the world. The firm was founded in the late 19th century by Eugene Van Ingen and the Mysore branch was founded in 1900, the company only closing in 1999 (although latterly it was mainly only existent in name). Van Ingen & Van Ingen had an almost unrivalled reputation for the quality of their taxidermy. At one point, the premises in Mysore had no fewer than 150 employees engaged in the preparation of specimens. Their skill in producing lifelike poses with trademark well-modelled ferocious faces was achieved by using high-quality moulds and mannequins. Their clients included royalty and nobility from around the world, even film stars, but the bulk of their orders were completed for the Maharajahs and Indian nobility. Their work is valued among collectors.

But Van Ingen's statistics begin to illustrate the scale on which animals were killed in the name of sport. Between 1875 and 1925 it's estimated that 80,000 tigers were killed in India. Van Ingen & Van Ingen alone processed 43,000 tigers during their 90 years in business. Over the years I've seen hunting diaries for 19th-century Indian expeditions that manifestly qualify this with literally thousands of dead animals listed and photographed by just one hunting party.

In 1947, when India gained its independence, hunters had a total free-for-all, killing most sorts of big game in huge quantities. When Indira Gandhi became Prime Minister in 1966 she endeavoured to save the fast-declining tiger. The export of skins was prohibited in 1969 and in 1971 tiger hunting was made illegal. This was only just in time, given that estimates at that point put the wild population in India at 1,800.

The current situation is not much better. With renewed poaching problems due to the Chinese medicine market and the demand for tiger bones, there are still fewer than 2,000 tigers left in the wild in India. Food for thought?

Miniature Marvel

What, you might think, do an MP, rampant homophobia and an imagined plot to undermine British society during the First World War have to do with a wonderful little camera? The answer is a man called Noel Pemberton Billing. Born in 1881, he was an early aviation pioneer who realised the importance of developing an air force. As an elected Member of Parliament at the beginning of the First World War, he strongly criticised the government for its lack of initiative in developing an air force separate from the army or navy. In his 1917 publication, *Air War and How to Wage It*, he ardently advocated the bombing of German cities. He also held decidedly right-wing views on issues such as homosexuality, a subject he pursued with much vigour, alleging a secret German plot to destabilise British society by 'exterminating the manhood of Britain'. This led to a sensational libel case in which he accused the actress Maud Allan of being a lesbian co-conspirator in the plot. He defended himself and won.

Billing founded the famous Supermarine aviation company and was also an innovative inventor. In 1936 he began work on a camera which was launched in 1937, known as the Compass. Despite Mr Billing's abhorrent views, it is a wonderful piece of aesthetically pleasing design. Machined from a solid block of aluminium, it is a classic: the Swiss army knife of the camera world. A camera so compact but bristling with so many technical innovations and functions that it required the Swiss watchmaker Jaeger-LeCoultre to manufacture it. Two versions were made – the Compass II came out in 1939 – and approximately 5,000 were manufactured in total up until 1941, when the war halted production. It was available with a selection of accessories. Today, a reasonable example will cost around £1,000 at auction but this is arguably very good value for such a wonderful piece of 1930s design.

The Compass camera – a design classic

In 1946, Billing designed another camera. Named the Phantom, it was never put into production. Christie's sold the unique prototype in 2001 and the 'come get me' estimate of £8,000–12,000 was soon shattered as it sailed to a record-breaking £146,750 including commission. It's a record that's now been broken on numerous occasions and not least by a wonderfully rare 1932 Leica II Luxus that I came across on the *Antiques Roadshow* about twelve years ago. It was one of only four ever made, its gilded body complete with the only known example of a crocodile skin case, and bearing the serial number 88840. The markets have moved considerably in the decade or so since I first saw it, mainly fuelled by Asian collectors, particularly the Chinese. I valued it at £5,000–8,000 at the time and that gradually increased over the years until extremely rare Leicas began realising hundreds of thousands of pounds. It was recently sold in Hong Kong for $620,000 (£380,000) although media expectations were higher. I am content that, at least for a while, it held the record for the highest value object ever sold after being featured on the *Antiques Roadshow*. Sometimes that which glisters is indeed gold.

The Leica II Luxus

Bombards and Black Jacks

I have several very old books in my library that are still to this day regarded as the definitive works on their subjects. *Blue Dash Chargers and Other Early English Tin Enamel Circular Dishes*, by Edward Downman, published in 1919, instantly springs to mind. Alas I don't have a copy of *Black Jacks and Leather Bottells; Being some account of leather drinking vessels in England and incidentally of other ancient vessels*, by Oliver Baker, published in 1921. At around £200 I don't think I'm likely to purchase one either, but it's this type of publication that emphasises the connoisseurial old-school character of certain collectors.

So, what is a 'bombard' or a 'black jack'? Essentially, they are vessels, jugs or pitchers made of leather, which have been used in various forms since quite early times; accurate references date from the 14th century. Meanwhile, 'bottells' – this is the correct spelling – are bulbous squat vessels with stoppers, used for water.

Such items are generally collected by those interested in vernacular items such as period oak furniture, brassware, pewter and the like, a market that used to be much more buoyant. Construction is of heavy stitched leather, usually lined with pitch and sometimes mounted with decorative silver or metal, other times emblazoned with heraldic arms or inscriptions.

The vessels were originally called 'jacks'; the term 'black jack' seems to have come into use in the 16th century, perhaps simply because of the colour but also, according to some scholars, to differentiate them in name from a number of other items referred to as jacks. Smaller vessels also known as jacks were made with straight sides and lined and mounted with silver rims. These are rarer and generally of richer construction.

Although fashioned in the same way, bombards were originally a much bigger vessel, holding a good six to eight gallons, weighty enough in leather but wholly unwieldy if made in pottery. They are variously mentioned in literature, including Shakespeare, often as a form of derisory remark! Apparently the name was derived from the similarity of the vessel to an early type of bulbous cannon. The terms bombard and black jack later became interchangeable. I was quite taken with the idea that the French, who had no tradition of using large leather flagons, apparently used to refer to Englishmen as 'drinking out of their bootes'.

Black jacks were generally a feature of communal eating. They held large quantities of ale or liquids and were useful in the refectories and halls of baronial houses and abbeys where the master and monks would eat together with their fellows or retinue. This tradition prevailed in the colleges and ancient establishments where, as objects, the jacks maintained an important status. The decline of the black jack was mainly due to changes in fashion. As the nobility began to eat separately, away from the household in their private 'dining rooms' the need for such large vessels diminished.

The value of black jacks has ridden the roller-coaster ride of fashionable demand in recent years. Values have been high and were particularly buoyant in the 1990s, yet recent results have shown a steady set of prices at a similar level to those realised in earlier heady days. Needless to say, those high prices did prompt a spate of forgeries and also the embellishment of originals with silver mounts and armorials designed to add appeal and more value. The fakers will never come close to the patina, texture and finish of a good 17th-century black jack but embellishments can be more difficult to spot. Add to this the fashion for adding spurious attributions in antiquity such as references to Oliver Cromwell and King Charles and the complexity of the field becomes obvious.

Brightwells of Leominster sold some honest examples recently: a pair of bombards for £3,800 and another jack for £2,300; but a more recent sale at Christie's South Kensington of the Ruud Bolmeijer collection saw some 34 lots of bombards, black jacks and bottells offered. The highest achiever, which realised £7,000 and bore an inscription on the silver mount to a 'Captain Gromio Pendarves 1765', reflected exactly the same price paid by the vendor in 2005. It also illustrates the financial incentive for fakers to dabble!

Fire Lizards

The Martin Brothers (*see* 'Ugly as Sin', *page 219*) are renowned for their eccentric wares, particularly the amazingly modelled 'Wally Birds', as we have seen. As with most studio output, many of the items are unique in their own way, being largely hand-made. So despite the fact that there are numerous 'Wally Birds', every example is different. However, a truly unique Martin Brothers duo came to light recently in the form of a pair of fire dogs (supports for fire tools). Unusually, they were made from ceramic and it seems highly likely that they were a special commission. Their form as two pairs of reptiles bound and seated back-to-back is typically quirky and it's likely a comment on the human condition. They pre-dated production of the famous 'Wally Birds' by some ten years but were obviously forerunners of the metaphorical nature of many Martin Brothers pieces.

Acquired by the vendor's family in the 1930s, they were described by Bonhams as 'important and unrecorded'. Speculation inferred that they may have been commissioned by one of the famous wealthy steel-making families from the Norwich/East Anglia region and the company Barnard, Bishop & Barnard, who were strong patrons of the Art and Crafts movement. Potential purchasers obviously agreed with their importance in the history of the art pottery movement and they made a pretty sparky £25,000 all-inclusive price.

❧❦❧

Dental Record

I hate paying for dental work. Following a recent visit to the surgery I was quoted £600 to have root canal treatment, which, frankly, I thought was too much. I bought a £7 tube of special toothpaste instead. The other option was to have the tooth extracted but the psychological trauma of the notion that I'm gradually heading towards a toothless old age put paid to that idea too. Yet, if I were as famous as John Lennon (God rest his soul) I might well have surrendered my whole headful of teeth if the price was guaranteed at the incredible £23,000 (including premium) that one of his molars sold for in 2011 at specialist entertainment auctioneers Omega in Stockport. The wisdom tooth had been given to his housekeeper Dorothy Jarlett.

At the time, the identity of the purchaser was unknown but he has since broken cover to announce his intentions for the tooth. Dentist Mr Michael Zuk from Alberta in Canada, said that he would like to extract the DNA sequence from Lennon's tooth and clone him.

Interviewed on BBC radio he said, 'Many people have thought about cloning famous people and I think John Lennon should be at the top of the heap' – although he did also say that it was just a matter of sitting around and waiting for the technology to improve.

Given this future possibility I wonder about the moral implications of us cloning all sorts of famous and infamous people from history based upon the parts of them housed in various collections all over the world. It makes me wonder about Napoleon's penis (in private ownership in the United States, as readers of my previous book *The Antiques Magpie* will know). It would also be rather worrying to find out that not all the parts represented the individuals they were meant to – and that the many mortal remains of Jesus that are held in reliquaries around the world might not herald a second coming but rather the accidental resurrection of a bunch of crucified criminals …

Balls Up

Given the shortage of legally available ivory, those in search of the raw material for carving objects go to great lengths to source supplies. Of course, much of this is achieved through the slaughter and poaching of elephants. However, one strange and perfectly legal way of acquiring it is through the purchase of antique ivory billiard balls.

Ivory has been used in early variations of snooker and billiards since the 17th century but it was during the 19th century that vast quantities of ivory were required to satisfy this increasingly popular sport. Given the size of the balls, it was difficult to make more than six or eight per tusk, meaning that the death of 10,000 elephants would produce around 40,000 sets of billiard balls. It's easy to do the maths. This situation was far from sustainable and even the manufacturers realised that their supply was seriously endangered.

Michael Phelan, an Irish-born American, was the most famous billiards player of the 19th century. His book, *Billiards Without a Master*, published in 1850, became a bestseller. He was involved in manufacturing equipment and endeavoured to standardise the game across the world. He was also the owner of several famous billiard parlours. Like his competitors, and bolstered by public concern, he realised that the supply of ivory was finite, and his company, Phelan & Collender, issued a challenge worth $10,000 to find a suitable substitute. There seems to be no evidence to show that the prize was ever awarded but various materials were substituted or invented, including celluloid and other plastic compounds. Modern balls are made of phenolic resins but the use of ivory persisted into the late 20th century, mainly in competitive events. As a result, there are still quite a few ivory billiard balls and, as a source of legal ivory, they are useful for carving everything from cane tops to netsuke and small okimonos. A quick scout around the net showed several sets which had sold for as much as £400 – for three balls.

❊⚘❊

Just the Ticket

I'm not a big racing man. An annual visit to Glorious Goodwood usually suffices, particularly if I'm invited to one of those rather exclusive boxes with waitress service and wonderful views across the course. Afterwards, when I return home, I attach the chic cut-card race badges to a pair of vintage binoculars or leave them dangling from the buttonhole of my linen suit to be discovered on the next occasion that I dress up for a race day. Suits are good like that: the pockets full of interesting markers always serve as a reminder of the last place you went to (or were not meant to be!).

In the 18th and 19th century, race badges or 'tickets' were often a more permanent affair and came in the form of silver, ivory or even ceramic ovals or roundels that were purchased by subscribers as personal admission passes. Similar tickets were also used for the opera and the theatre and they are now highly collectable. In a recent sale held by Dee Atkinson & Harrison of Driffield in East Yorkshire I was intrigued by a couple of silver tickets that were issued by the Beverley racecourse in 1767 at the inception of an annual meet. Prior to that, occasional races had been held but these were part of a 330-ticket offering sold to members to raise £1,000 for a new stand on the Westwood pasture. One of the tickets was engraved 'Rev'd Gee' – a steward of the course – and numbered 46. The other was numbered 88 and engraved with the initials 'RS', thought to be for a Richard Stern.

The slightly meagre estimates of £100–200 each were soon surpassed and the former made a competitive £2,800 and the latter a winning £3,300. What really won me over to the charms of these particular tickets was the fact that the current Beverley Race Company had kindly offered three years' free admission to the buyers – a rather nice historic footnote to a story that began almost 250 years ago.

D-Day Deception

Wars throughout history have frequently been littered with clever tales of deception, ingenious sleights of hand and schemes designed to deflect the enemy's attention away from critical battle strategies and invasions. There are many instances in the Second World War of successful and intriguing plans to outmanoeuvre the enemy (*see* 'Jolly Roger', *page 72*), although in these days of complicated electronic counter-espionage and surveillance, many seem laughably home-spun and simplistic.

I'm sure many of you have seen the 1959 film *The Longest Day*, starring John Wayne, Richard Burton and Henry Fonda. Although jazzed up for Hollywood, there is a part of the film where an actual event is portrayed whereby a number of dummies are parachuted from aircraft to deceive the Nazis into thinking that a larger force of paratroopers are being dropped in a particular area. The celluloid versions of these 'paradummies' are quite realistic-looking figures but in reality the dummies were made of sackcloth or hessian filled with wool, sand and sawdust and were under 3ft tall. They were known as 'Ruperts' after the slang name used for British officers and several hundred were dropped on 5–6 June 1944 at the D-Day landings. Apparently, the 'paradummies' were accompanied by several real parachutists who added to the realism of the action, which went by the name Operation Titanic.

Although one had been sold by Hermann Historica of Munich in 2009 for around £1,700, these rarely come up for sale and the scarce appearance of an example at Marlow's of Stafford brought enough attention for it to raise a reasonable £900. However, nothing is new; the Germans had used a similar decoy device when they invaded Holland in 1940, and the Americans also had their own smarter-looking version (just like the GIs) which was nicknamed 'Oscar'. The Americans have subsequently used them in several campaigns, including Vietnam and the Gulf War. Another ruse that they also apparently pursued against the Vietcong was to parachute in blocks of ice, which would obviously melt, leaving the enemy guessing about the whereabouts of the paratrooper!

Zig-Zag

I have a good Dutch friend who is an architect. He has often recounted the story of how his family once owned two chairs by the iconic Dutch designer and architect Gerrit Thomas Rietveld. Born in 1888, Rietveld was the son of a joiner and initially set up his own furniture workshop in

1917. It was there, in the same year, that the famous 'Red and Blue' chair was designed, although it was not initially painted in the characteristic Mondrian style now familiar from glossy coffee-table books.

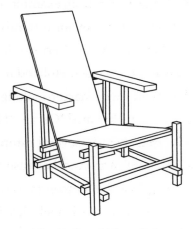

The Red and Blue chair

The chair evolved after Rietveld joined the 'De Stijl' movement in 1919, the year that he qualified as an architect. The movement broadened his access to foreign opportunities and he was invited to exhibit at the Bauhaus by its founder Walter Gropius. Rietveld's most famous commission is the 1924 Reitveld Schröder House in Utrecht, now a UNESCO World Heritage Site.

His break with the De Stijl movement in 1928 fostered an association with a more functional style known as Nieuwe Bouwen and he became predominantly occupied with cheap prefabricated social housing projects. In 1934 he designed another iconic seating solution known as the 'Zig-Zag' chair. It's here that my friend starts to bemoan the loss of his family's two Rietveld masterpieces: in 2011, Christie's sold a period pine example for €18,750. A child's version was more recently sold for £14,000!

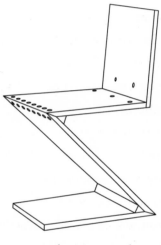

The Zig-Zag chair

Cape of Good Hope

There are many romantic stories of wounded soldiers falling in love with their nurses and carers. It's not a great stretch of the imagination to understand why. No doubt there also were many sad stories of those who were never able to realise their feelings. One particularly emotive manifestation of this situation are the Second World War nurses' capes adorned on their trademark red interiors with the numerous military, naval and air force 'tiles', badges and insignia of patients and colleagues that the nurses collected during their encounters in service. In many ways, these were a popular fashion statement among the women but I can't help feeling that they probably meant so much more to the nurses who wore them and the people who gave them. They are, however, now highly collectable and I was fascinated to find one on eBay with no fewer than 117 insignia sewn on to it; what's more, it had belonged to an interesting lady by the name of Barbara Mary Stoney. She had served with the Voluntary Aid Detachment (VAD) and was the first and only official biographer of Enid Blyton, the children's author. Coincidentally, she also wrote the biography of Noel Pemberton Billing, the designer of the Compass camera mentioned earlier in this book (*see* 'Miniature Marvel', *page 278*).

Although another fine example of a similar cape with no fewer than 150 badges had been sold by C&T Auctions online some months earlier for £1,400, the provenance of this one obviously helped it to climb to a worthy online sale price of £1,850. This was also a positive reflection of the interest that online sales sites can garner from serious collectors.

EPILOGUE

It's been an interesting year. In a world that's very value driven and where success is often measured by percentages sold and values attained, I have learnt to take a more relaxed view of what 'success' actually means these days. I enjoy the variety, the worthless mixed with the worthwhile, the right to decide whether it's of value to me, rather than it having to be rationally defined in terms of a monetary value that the market understands. It's often frustrating having to be the apologist for what the market dictates (or doesn't understand) rather than what you feel an object should really be worth – but after all, this is the joy of collecting, the eternal pursuit of the rare or the valuable *or* the objects that primarily tick the boxes for *you*.

This is the point. The word 'valuable' means different things to different people, as does 'rare'. Evaluating the worth of a Michelangelo or an old bus ticket is one of those elusive ideas that fascinates me, the notion that an art dealer at the top of his game might consider the collector of bus tickets to be preoccupied with a rather trifling obsession, but at the same time be happy to pay a huge amount for a collage because Kurt Schwitters stuck a similar bus ticket to a melee of magazine cut-outs. Simplistic? Perhaps. But that's the eternal conundrum of art and collecting: there are so many esoteric facets to it that 'value' cannot be judged merely by the physical manifestation of the object itself. You only have to look at the numerous examples within this almanac that highlight those who didn't understand the magnetism of what they held, the desirability it possessed for others. So given all these arcane, abstract and rarefied reasons, it is on occasion almost impossible to actually predict what some items are worth and this is why this is such a captivating world to work in.

To me, the joy of being a generalist is really quite obvious. The need to tap into all those capillaries of history that lead you through the veins of discovery and on to the arteries of fulfilment were part of the pathway to a kind of cerebral consummation. However, it's a goal that you never really achieve because the goalposts are constantly moved along the touchline of your life, pushing you into different fields of interest and emotional interpretation. Year in and year out, the world of art and antiques generates the material that continually tops up that system. It is the lifeblood of my world and I look forward to gleaning the best nuggets for *Allum's Antiques Almanac 2016*.

Marc Allum

ACKNOWLEDGEMENTS

There's a game that a couple of friends play with me. They pick a subject totally at random and I have to match a story to it – without hesitation. The fact is, I'm very good at it, probably because I seem to have spent my life inadvertently collecting tall tales and copious amounts of fairly useless information. Or is it useless? Apparently not, because for all the light-hearted ribbing I suffer, this data seems to have come in pretty useful over the years both professionally and socially. In fact, it actually provides me with quite a reasonable living. Luckily, part of that living is provided by the lovely people at Icon Books who allow me to indulge my insatiable curiosity for the quirkier side of art and antiques in the form of books. Strangely, every time I write a book I swear I'm not going to pen another but being an author is like being hooked on drugs. Finding those words is like hunting for a factual fix; running out is tantamount to going cold turkey – the roller coaster of deadlines and the nervous sweats of writer's block haunt you through your twilight hours and, finally, when the book goes to the printers a sense of loss and exhaustion ensues as the publishers take possession and send it out into the world to take its chances among the myriad of other publications, only for the media equivalent of Alcoholics Anonymous to send you on a crazy recovery course of literary festivals, lectures and radio interviews. Yet that joyous feeling of signing on the dotted contract line is still a high – thank you Icon.

So, despite the inevitable hardships of shoe-horning my literary commitments into a hectic schedule I couldn't do it without the support of the many friends and work colleagues to whom I dedicate this book. From my workmates and supporters on the BBC *Antiques Roadshow*, the editors of the many magazines who have commissioned me, the countless people in the auction world who have given me both work and inspiration, I am eternally grateful. To my family, I can only apologise. At times it may not seem like it but committing my thoughts to paper is a kind of cathartic release, so your patience is always greatly appreciated.

In short, I love it – writing, that is – but without my innate curiosity there would be no *Allum's Antiques Almanac*.

Marc Allum

APPENDIX

A HANDPICKED SELECTION OF INTERESTING SOCIETIES

The Pylon Appreciation Society
www.pylons.org
The National Heritage Ironwork Group
www.nhig.org.uk
The Pillbox Study Group (Second World War pillboxes)
www.pillbox-study-group.org.uk
The Antique Poison Bottle Collectors Club
www.poisonbottleclub.org
Society for Clay Pipe Research
www.dawnmist.org.uk
The Church Monuments Society
www.churchmonumentssociety.org
The British Association for Cemeteries in South Asia
www.bacsa.org.uk
The Brewery History Society
www.breweryhistory.com
The King James Bible Trust
www.kingjamesbibletrust.org
The List and Index Society
www.listandindexsociety.org.uk

The Battlefields Trust
  www.battlefieldstrust.com
The Ghostsigns Project
  www.ghostsigns.co.uk
The Wallpaper History Society
  www.wallpaperhistorysociety.org.uk
The Ancient Yew Group
  www.ancient-yew.org
The Test Card Circle
  www.testcardcircle.org.uk
The Drinking Fountain Association
  www.drinkingfountains.org
Airfields of Britain Conservation Trust
  www.abct.org.uk
The Regional Furniture Society
  www.regionalfurnituresociety.com
The Computer Conservation Society
  www.computerconservationsociety.org
The Richard III Society
  www.richardiii.net
The Branch Line Society
  www.branchline.org.uk
The Traditional Paint Forum
  www.traditionalpaintforum.org.uk
The Naval Dockyards Society
  www.navaldockyards.org
Dating Old Welsh Houses Group
  www.datingoldwelshhouses.co.uk
The Waterway Recovery Group
  www.waterways.org.uk/wrg/
The National Association of Mining History Organisations
  www.namho.org

The Ranulf Higden Society (devoted to the eponymous
Benedictine monk [1299–1364] and author of *Polychronicon*, a
seven-volume history of the world)
www.ranulfhigden.org.uk/
The Pre-Raphaelite Society
www.pre-raphaelitesociety.org
The International Society for the Study of Pilgrimage Art
peregrinations.kenyon.edu/vol2-2_1/welcome.html
The International Society of Meccanomen
www.internationalmeccanomen.org.uk

BIBLIOGRAPHY

General Resources Consulted

Oxford English Dictionary, Oxford University Press, online access, 2014.

www.wikipedia.org

www.camerapedia.wikia.com

www.britannica.com

www.brainyquote.com (quotes)

www.goodreads.com (quotes)

www.newguineaart.com (quotes)

Sources Regarding Specific Entries

WEBSITES

http://www.dreweatts.com/cms/pages/lot/13719/72 (Thangka Lot)

http://www.antiquestradegazette.com/news/2013/nov/12/thangka-
leads-dreweatts-asian-art-sale-at-450000/ (Thangka Lot)

http://en.wikipedia.org/wiki/Buddhism (Thangka Lot)

http://politicalassassinations.com/2013/09/famed-oswald-window/
(Assassin's Ring)

http://www.telegraph.co.uk/news/worldnews/northamerica/
usa/4797812/Ownership-of-Lee-Harvey-Oswald-sniper-window
-through-which-he-shot-JFK-contested.html (Assassin's Ring)

http://www.dallasnews.com/news/jfk50/20131024-lee-harvey-oswald-
s-wedding-ring-fetches-108000-at-auction.ece (Assassin's Ring)

http://olympic-museum.de/torches/torch1948.htm (Holding a Torch)

http://en.wikicollecting.org/top-10-olympic-games-memorabilia-
most-expensive-sold-auction (Holding a Torch)

http://www.mirror.co.uk/news/real-life-stories/how-mirror-challenge-
nearly-defeated-2339698 (All Tied Up)

Bibliography

http://www.dreweatts.com/cms/pages/lot/36106/47 (All Tied Up)

http://money.cnn.com/2013/11/18/news/economy/rare-coin-auction/ (Crystal Ball)

http://www.theguardian.com/commentisfree/2014/feb/16/art-market-auctions-records-global-economy (Art Market Matters)

http://www.theguardian.com/artanddesign/2013/nov/13/francis-bacon-lucian-freud-geniuses (Art Market Matters)

https://www.bonhams.com/auctions/21427/lot/11/ (Derby Day)

http://news.bbc.co.uk/1/hi/in_pictures/4094801.stm (Derby Day)

https://www.bonhams.com/auctions/20085/lot/2004/ (Derby Day)

http://www.christies.com/lotfinder/lot/charlie-chaplinthe-great-dictator-4413537-details.aspx?intObjectID=4413537 (Derby Day)

http://news.yahoo.com/blogs/odd-news/figurine-found-in-attic-sells-for--5-million-214652285.html (Lapidary Legend)

http://www.fabergeresearch.com/eggsframe.php (Lapidary Legend)

http://www.telegraph.co.uk/culture/art/art-news/10706025/The-20m-Faberge-egg-that-was-almost-sold-for-scrap.html (Lapidary Legend)

http://www.theguardian.com/culture/2013/oct/10/cheapside-hoard-treasure-byzantium-london-museum (Not on the Cheapside)

http://www.bbc.co.uk/news/world-us-canada-25115524 (The Printed Word)

http://www.bbc.co.uk/news/entertainment-arts-24215647 (Without Prejudice)

http://www.jane-austens-house-museum.org.uk/index.php (Without Prejudice)

http://www.crowsauctions.co.uk/news/ (Stovepipe)

http://www.paulfrasercollectibles.com/News/Unique-Items/Brunel's-silver-snuff-box-achieves-700pc-increase-in-UK-auction/12680.page#.UoUfgfldV8E (Stovepipe)

http://www.antiquestradegazette.com/news/2013/dec/19/house-prices-are-soaring/ (Property Bubble)

http://www.woolleyandwallis.co.uk/news/%C2%A35-bet-brings-%C2%A363,440.aspx (The £5 Raindrop)

http://www.mirror.co.uk/news/world-news/pink-star-worlds-most-expensive-2791994 (Star Lot)

Bibliography

https://uk.finance.yahoo.com/news/pink-star-diamond-sells-world-record-auction-sothebys-204932463--finance.html (Star Lot)

http://www.coinworks.com.au (Holey Grail)

http://www.esquire.com/blogs/culture/damien-hirst-end-of-money-as-pure-art-14950053 (Past Picassos)

http://www.antimonide.com/2008/10/24/lee-miller-jeu-de-paume-paris/ (Past Picassos)

http://www.antiquestradegazette.com/news/2013/oct/04/matteo-sellas-guitar-strikes-a-%C2%A348,000-chord/ (Axe Hero)

http://www.dailymail.co.uk/news/article-2381685/Salvador-Dali-brooch-The-Eye-Time-sells-eye-watering-auction.html (Eye Eye)

https://www.salvador-dali.org/museus/en_index.html (Eye Eye)

http://www.dailymail.co.uk/news/article-2399999/Christopher-Dresser-teapot-used-family-years-1879-prototype-worth-20-000.html (Dresser Designs)

http://www.bbc.co.uk/news/entertainment-arts-27230586 (Face to Face)

http://www.antiquestradegazette.com/news/2013/aug/05/the-toast-of-trelissick-house-sale-at-32000/ (Me Old China)

http://www.mingtombs.eu/i/gen/general.html (Who Pays the Ferryman)

http://blog.wellcomelibrary.org/2014/01/the-enigma-of-the-medieval-almanac/ (Not Allum's Almanac)

http://www.wilkinsons-auctioneers.co.uk (Base Metal)

http://www.shipwreck.net/ (Base Metal)

http://www.independent.co.uk/news/uk/home-news/in-too-deep-warship-wreck-bounty-hunter-under-scrutiny-from-britains-marine-watchdog-8906374.html (Base Metal)

http://www.museumsassociation.org/museums-journal/news/29072013-stamp-auction-falls-short-of-target-british-postal-museum-sothebys (Stamp of Disapproval)

https://www.google.co.uk/search?q=gavin+littaur&rlz=1C1GGGE_en-gbGB481GB481&oq=gavin+littaur&aqs=chrome..69i57j0l3.3192j0j8&sourceid=chrome&es_sm=122&ie=UTF-8 (Stamp of Disapproval)

http://www.bowlofchalk.net/things-are-afoot/temple-bar-the-gate-that-moved-twice (Gatekeeper)

Bibliography

http://www.liveauctioneers.com/item/17877941_a-charles-ii-carved-oak-gate-top-rail-circa-1669 (Gatekeeper)

http://www.dailymail.co.uk/news/article-2483589/Skull-crossbones-flag-WW2s-HMS-Seraph-emerges.html (Jolly Roger)

http://www.bbc.co.uk/news/uk-25128666 (Play Misty for Me)

http://www.paulfrasercollectibles.com/News/Art-%26-Photography/Christie's-scores-World-Record-price-at-auction-for-a-Cycladic-marble-figure/5415.page (Grave Decision)

http://www.telegraph.co.uk/culture/art/artsales/9641190/Market-news-Ancient-Egyptian-work-of-art-sets-world-record-at-Christies.html (Grave Decision)

http://www.irishexaminer.com/ireland/rare-3000-year-old-golden-torc-unveiled-to-the-public-in-belfast-237309.html (Torc of the Town)

http://www.getty.edu/art/gettyguide/artObjectDetails?artobj=64649 (Yankee Doodle)

http://www.bbc.co.uk/news/uk-england-wiltshire-24582739 (A Big Fiddle)

http://www.dailymail.co.uk/news/article-2465997/Worlds-English-newspaper-expected-fetch-15-000-auctioned-350-years-published.html (Headline News)

http://www.dailymail.co.uk/news/article-2076750/Barbara-Hepworth-statue-stolen-metal-thieves-Dulwich-Park-south-London.html (Scrap Metal)

http://www.theguardian.com/artanddesign/2009/may/17/henry-moore-sculpture-theft-reclining-figure (Scrap Metal)

http://www.bbc.co.uk/news/uk-scotland-south-scotland-24511737 (Scrap Metal)

http://www.huffingtonpost.com/2013/04/29/1000-bill-auction-world-record_n_3178845.html (Banknote)

http://mentalfloss.com/article/53557/10-most-expensive-coins-and-banknotes-world (Banknote)

http://www.bluejohnstone.com/ (Blue John)

http://www.candtauctions.co.uk/rare-corgi-no-261-james-bond-aston-martin-db5-taken-from-the-film-goldfinger-unopened-trade-pack-2/ (Goldfinger)

Bibliography

http://www.telegraph.co.uk/news/obituaries/9998590/Marcel-van-Cleemput.html (Goldfinger)

http://www.christies.com/lotfinder/books-manuscripts/smith-adam-an-inquiry-into-the-5370984-details.aspx (Boom or Bust)

http://www.theguardian.com/world/2008/nov/05/naaman-diller-israeli-clock-thief (Clock Watcher)

http://www.chippenham.gov.uk/files/Downloads/CVIC/SPRING2013%20FINAL.pdf (Old Cow)

http://www.antiquetoyworld.com/auctions/storming-finish-to-the-vectis-2011-military-civilian-figures-equipment-and-accessories-sale-season/ (Old Cow)

http://www.bonhams.com/auctions/19796/lot/57/ (Sword Play)

http://www.bonhams.com/auctions/19796/lot/78/ (Sword Play)

http://www.worldmuseumofman.org/display.php?item=814 (Sword Play)

http://www.fischerauktionen.ch/ueber/highlights.aspx?oid=35944 (Sword Play)

http://www.telegraph.co.uk/culture/tvandradio/10540670/Fiona-Bruce-helps-priest-turn-400-into-a-fortune.html (Van's the Man)

http://www.gjsaville-caricatures.co.uk (Alter Ego)

http://store.paulfrasercollectibles.com/famous-hair-s/1830.htm?searching=Y&sort=13&cat=1830&show=9&page=4 (Hair Today Gone Tomorrow)

http://www.dance-enthusiast.com/features/view/Marie-Taglioni-The-Instant-Ballerina-2010-03-23 (Ballet Buffet)

http://www.bbc.co.uk/news/technology-22667353 (Slice of Apple)

http://www.telegraph.co.uk/technology/steve-jobs/10380351/Steve-Jobs-hand-built-1976-Apple-1-computer-at-auction.html (Slice of Apple)

http://www.fritzhansen.com/en/designers/christian-dell (Haus Design)

http://www.paulfrasercollectibles.com/News/Eva-Peron's-brooch-achieves-$461,000-at-Christie's/15360.page#.U5B35fmwLYg (Flag Day)

http://jamesbond.ajb007.co.uk/rolex-submariner/ (Watch This)

http://www.bloomberg.com/news/2013-11-11/rolex-daytona-sells-for-record-1-1-million-at-christie-s.html (Watch This)

https://www.flickr.com/photos/topcat_angel/2343618575/ (Chocoholic)

http://www.readex.com/blog/civil-war-imagery-clipper-ship-sailing-cards (We Are Sailing)

http://www.theguardian.com/world/2013/sep/18/martin-luther-kings-secretary-historic-documents (The Price of Freedom)

http://www.paulfrasercollectibles.com/News/Martin-Luther-King's-Dexter-Avenue-address-notecards-realise-$31,500/15400.page#.U5R56vldV8E (The Price of Freedom)

http://news.bbc.co.uk/onthisday/hi/dates/stories/june/11/newsid_3726000/3726535.stm (The Master)

http://www.bonhams.com/press_release/14104/ (The Master)

http://www.bloomberg.com/news/2013-10-02/ferrari-gto-becomes-most-expensive-car-at-52-million.html (The Master)

http://dartmed.dartmouth.edu/spring03/html/exhuming_bonaparte.shtml (Napoleon's Noisette)

http://www.theedinburghreporter.co.uk/2013/06/napoleons-table-to-be-sold-by-edinburgh-auctioneers/ (Napoleon's Noisette)

http://politicalquotes.org (Completely Jaded)

http://most-expensive.com/pearl (Pearl Jam)

http://www.vam.ac.uk/content/exhibitions/exhibition-pearls/about-the-exhibition/ (Pearl Jam)

http://www.vam.ac.uk/content/articles/w/wolsey-angels-appeal/ (Angels of Death)

www.grafittiartist.com (Bank On It)

http://www.bbc.co.uk/news/entertainment-arts-24518315 (Bank On It)

http://the10mostknown.com/top-10-famous-graffiti-artists-2/ (Bank On It)

http://obeliskseven.blogspot.co.uk/2010/11/london-1917-night-of-terror-for.html (Bombing Mission)

http://www.omgfacts.com/History/The-top-of-the-Empire-State-building-was/52166 (Bombing Mission)

https://www.bonhams.com/auctions/21122/lot/1013/ (Cracking Lot)

Bibliography

http://www.nutcrackermuseum.com/ (Cracking Lot)

http://www.bonhams.com/auctions/11282/lot/117/ (Good Sir Toby)

http://www.nlm.nih.gov/hmd/almanac/heyday.html (Quack Cure)

http://immigrants1900.weebly.com/jobs.html (Quack Cure)

http://www.wiltshirebusinessonline.co.uk/news/10305848.Human_
skulls_for_sale_at_auction/?ref=ar (Auction Sniper)

http://www.dailymail.co.uk/news/article-2513246/Apollo-1-lunar-
Bible-collection-taken-moon-sells-130-000.html (Apollo Apostles)

http://www.christianpost.com/news/lunar-bible-that-went-to-moon-
fetches-75k-at-dallas-auction-119846/ (Apollo Apostles)

http://www.businessinsider.com/the-20-most-outrageous-luxury-
purchases-in-may-2012-5?op=1 (Apollo Apostles)

http://www.telegraph.co.uk/culture/books/9727907/From-Kafka-
with-fear.html (Mouse Man)

http://www.bodleian.ox.ac.uk/news/2011-april-04 (Mouse Man)

http://www.newyorker.com/online/blogs/culture/2013/11/
the-knoedler-and-company-rothko-fake.html (Fakes and Fortune)

http://www.theguardian.com/artanddesign/2014/apr/22/forged-art-
scandal-new-york-artist-china-spain (Fakes and Fortune)

http://artdaily.com/news/63049/Bonhams-sells-100--of-French-
champagnery-s-gold-coin-treasure#.U8ft7PldV8E (Golden Shower)

http://www.bonhams.com/auctions/20922/lot/254/ (Poetic Stuff)

http://www.hamhigh.co.uk/news/fragment_of_keats_poem_sells_
for_world_record_breaking_price_at_bonhams_auction_1_2020896
(Poetic Stuff)

http://www.blouinartinfo.com/news/story/903077/christies-rakes-in-
495-million-the-highest-total-for-any-art (Moon River)

http://www.christies.com/about/press-center/releases/pressrelease.
aspx?pressreleaseid=6163 (Moon River)

http://www.sothebys.com/en/auctions/2013/so-williams-n08984.html
#&page=all&sort=lotNum-asc&viewMode=list (Moon River)

http://www.forbes.com/sites/hannahelliott/2010/10/26/inside-the-
louis-vuitton-special-order-workshop/ (Traveller's Friend)

http://www.thegoldsmiths.co.uk/media/3751010/ashleyrussell.pdf
(Fork and Knife)

http://www.antiquestradegazette.com/news/2014/jun/27/a-%C2%A
325,000-record-for-irish-flatware/ (Fork and Knife)

http://www.christies.com/lotfinder/lot/a-charles-ii-gold-trefid-
spoon-mark-3829194-details.aspx?intObjectID=3829194 (Fork and
Knife)

http://www.silverflatware.co.uk/patterns.html (Fork and Knife)

http://www.nationalhorsebrasssociety.org.uk/Core/Horse-Brass/
Pages/terrets_swingers-1506.aspx (Muck and Brass)

http://collectorshorsebrasses.weebly.com/hameplates.html (Muck and
Brass)

http://www.tsauction.co.uk/2013/11/the-autumn-reading-carriage-
heavy-horse-sale-including-horse-brasses/ (Muck and Brass)

http://www.woolleyandwallis.co.uk/news/martin-brothers-bird-
breaks-previous-record.aspx (Ugly as Sin)

http://www.pylons.org/ (Odd Societies)

www.peregrinations.kenyon.edu/vol2-2_1/welcome.html (Odd
Societies)

http://boardgamegeek.com/boardgame/21926/new-and-fashionable-
game-jew (Game Off!)

http://www.historic-memphis.com/memphis/black-americana/black-
americana.html (Game Off!)

http://www.bankofengland.co.uk/banknotes/pages/about/faqs.aspx
(Promise to Pay)

http://www.bonhams.com/press_release/11252/ (Chelsea Boot)

http://jimsworldandwelcometoit.com/tag/beatles/ (Chelsea Boot)

http://www.jamesdeanartifacts.com/ (Chelsea Boot)

http://www.bonhams.com/auctions/19801/lot/304/?list_search_
query=1&lang=en_gb&back_to_year=2003&sale_no=19801
&limit=9999&query=boots&create_facets=False&page_anchor=
q1_1%3Dboots%26m1%3D1%26b1%3Dlist%26MR1_page_lots
%3D2%26r1%3D10 (Chelsea Boot)

http://brunoclaessens.com/blog/2014/03/r-i-p-jean-willy-mestach-
1926-2014/#.U9Zvz_ldV8E (Tall Story)

http://www.christies.com/lotfinder/lot/a-french-papier-mache-
bulldog-4495022-details.aspx?intObjectID=4495022 (Bulldog Blues)

http://winelabelcircle.org/labels (Label Freak)

Bibliography

http://www.antiquestradegazette.com/news/2013/mar/21/
the-captains-prize-spice-box-makes-10500/ (Stolen Goods)

http://www.sworder.co.uk/index.php?_a=viewProd&productId=50175
(Owls of Shame)

http://history1900s.about.com/od/1950s/a/firstcreditcard.htm
(Credit Crunch)

http://english.stackexchange.com/questions/39092/how-did-sinister-
the-latin-word-for-left-handed-get-its-current-meaning (Touched by
the Devil)

http://www.guitarworld.com/interview-roger-mayer-secrets-jimi-
hendrixs-guitar-setup (Touched by the Devil)

http://www.telegraph.co.uk/news/celebritynews/2684648/Scorched-
Jimi-Hendrix-guitar-sells-for-280000.html (Touched by the Devil)

http://wallacelive.wallacecollection.org/eMuseumPlus?service=
ExternalInterface&module=collection&objectId=61534&viewType
=detailView (Sporting Life)

http://windlegends.org/crossbow.htm (Sporting Life)

http://www.antiques-info.co.uk/only-surviving-poppy-sells-to-maker-
of-the-victoria-cross-2171.php (Sole Survivor)

http://www.grandlodgescotland.com/index.php/masonic-subjects/
robert-burns (Serious Burns)

http://www.amazon.com/s/ref=sr_pg_1?rh=n%3A4991425011
%2Cn%3A219147426011%2Cn%3A219147428011%2Cn%3
A9243922011&ie=UTF8&qid=1407869610&ajr=2 (In God We
Trust)

http://time.com/13071/saddle-ridge-hoard-gold-coins/ (In God We
Trust)

http://www.hmsrichmond.org/avast/customs.htm (Whipped Up)

http://www.mirror.co.uk/news/uk-news/king-edward-viii-foul-
mouthed-handwritten-2851508 (Rude Letter)

http://www.antiquestradegazette.com/news/2012/jul/27/marklin-
paddle-steamer-brings-record-as-claus-sale-sails-to-18m-/ (Ship
Shape)

http://www.sothebys.com/en/auctions/2013/the-cunliffe-musk-
mallow-palace-bowl-hk0493/cunliffe-musk-mallow-palace-
bowl/2013/09/cunliffe-musk-mallow-palace-bowl.html (Palace Bowl)

Bibliography

http://newswatch.nationalgeographic.com/2014/03/10/a-concise-history-of-tiger-hunting-in-india/ (Ivory Tower)

http://www.takepart.com/article/2014/06/05/good-news-elephants-antiques-roadshow-will-finally-stop-featuring-ivory-tusks (Ivory Tower)

http://www.dailymail.co.uk/news/article-2579658/Princes-call-destroy-royal-ivory-treasures-echo-Nazis-Antiques-Roadshow-expert-blasts-William.html (Ivory Tower)

http://www.fws.gov/international/travel-and-trade/ivory-ban-questions-and-answers.html (Ivory Tower)

http://www.royalcollection.org.uk/microsites/vandahl/MicroObject.asp?item=0&themeid=731&object=1561&row=0&detail=magnify (Ivory Tower)

http://www.ephotozine.com/article/the-world-s-most-expensive-camera-121 (Miniature Marvel)

http://camerapedia.wikia.com/wiki/Compass (Miniature Marvel)

http://www.worldcollectorsnet.com/articles/black-jacks-bombards-antique-drinking-vessels/ (Bombards and Black Jacks)

http://www.bonhams.com/auctions/20815/lot/3/ (Fire Lizards)

http://www.dailymail.co.uk/news/article-2400142/Dentist-Michael-Zuk-hopes-use-John-Lennons-rotten-tooth-CLONE-Beatle.html (Dental Record)

http://www.tfquilty43.com/catalog/product_info.php?products_id=62 (D-Day Deception)

http://www.telegraph.co.uk/news/uknews/6262848/D-day-dummy-to-be-sold.html (D-Day Deception)

http://www.christies.com/lotfinder/furniture-lighting/a-pine-zig-zag-chair-designed-by-gerrit-5415030-details.aspx (Zig-Zag)

http://www.ebay.co.uk/itm/WW2-VAD-Nurse-039-s-Cape-with-cloth-formation-badges-inc-SAS-Glider-Pilot-Indian-/400612590533 (Cape of Good Hope)

Picture acknowledgements

The Charlie Chaplin image, page 16, is from Getty Images.

The image on page 52, from *Street Life of London*, is from LSE Library's collections, SR1146.

The $1,000 bill on page 92 is courtesy of the National
Numismatic Collection at the Smithsonian Institution.

The drawings on pages 101–2, 118, 252, 293 and 294 are by
Nicholas Halliday.

Thanks to Robert Opie for supplying the images on pages 110
and 147.

The picture of Harrowden Hall on page 164 is from *Country Life*.
Thanks also to Robert Wharton at Wellingborough Museum for
helping to locate a suitable image.

Finally, thanks to Dr James Wilkes for supplying the Martin
Brothers image on page 220.

USEFUL TRADE AND INDUSTRY LINKS

Antiques are Green, www.antiquesaregreen.org

Antiques News, www.antiquesnews.co.uk

Confédération Internationale des Négociants en Oeuvres d'Art, www.cinoa.org

International Interior Design Association, www.iida.org

The Antique Collectors Club (Antique Collecting Magazine), www.antique-collecting.co.uk

The Antiques Trade Gazette (ATG), www.antiquestradegazette.com

The British Antique Dealers Association (BADA), www.bada.org

The Association of Art & Antiques Dealers (LAPADA), www.lapada.org

The British Antique Furniture Restorer's Association, www.bafra.org.uk

The Antique Dealers Association of America, www.adadealers.com

The Society of Fine Art Auctioneers & Valuers, www.sofaa.info

The National Association of Decorative & Fine Arts Societies, www.nadfas.org.uk

The British Hallmarking Council, www.bis.gov.uk/britishhallmarkingcouncil

The Antiques Magpie

From the mythical artefacts of the ancient world to saucy seaside postcards, *The Antiques Magpie* explores the wonderful world of antiques and collectables.

With *Antiques Roadshow* regular Marc Allum as your guide, go in search of stolen masterpieces, learn the secrets of the forgers, track down Napoleon's toothbrush and meet the garden gnome insured for £1 million.

Eclectic, eccentric and brimming with remarkable tales from history, this book is for all those who are fascinated by the relics of the past.

'Not only a very useful overall guide for collectors ... and a source of unlikely information, but a laugh a page. A perfect present for virtually everyone.' *Country Life*

ISBN: 9781848317420 (paperback)/
9781848316195 (ebook)